TERMINAL FICTION

Selected Lyrics and Words
(1995-2017)

ADOLF N.S.

Terminal House Press

CONTENTS

THE MARAUDING BAND OF CUT-THROATS

FOREWORD

Terminal Fiction is a collection of selected lyrics and words that I wrote between 1995 and 2017. It includes lyrics to songs that I wrote for my solo projects and bands – Cori Celesti, A.N.S., and Raygun Circus – as well as for other projects and bands, like The Marauding Band of Cut-Throats, T.O.E., and Tactical Fever. The lyrics in this collection are arranged in chronological order by release. The year that appears after the lyrics indicates when they were written, followed by the title of the release they are from. In cases where the lyrics appear in more than one release, the release that the lyrics first appear in is used. I have also included selections from *The Village,* a pre-Cori Celesti album from 1996 that I recorded under the name of Yestehi. The Uncollected Lyrics and Words section at the end of this collection includes lyrics and words that I wrote but never used, as well as lyrics to songs that were never recorded, including lyrics written for T.O.E. and Tactical Fever.

Adolf N.S. – San Diego, May 2019

TERMINAL
FICTION

CORI CELESTI

CORI CELESTI

RELEASES

The Village (1996)

Perfect World (1997)

Britvaica Risen (1998)

Vinegar Dreams in the Puppet Tree (Video Two) (1998)

The Mandorla Device (1999)

The Morning After... (1999)

Video One (1995-1997) (1999)

Video Three (1999)

Foxtrot Leviathan (2000)

A Miner Stripped (2000)

Video Four (2000)

Man of a Thousand Ecstasies (2000)

Only Darkness Has the Power (2000)

The Lincoln Caper (2000)

The Letter Killeth (2001)

In the Animal Garden (2001)

Postcards from Oblivion (2002)

Like Pineapples in a Hothouse (2003)

A Sense of Urgency (2003)

All's Well That Ends Well (2013)

WHITE SHEET

when the scorching brimstone
of this concrete pit
and ignorant albatross
flee from the lips
take leave of the meadow
of crass razorblades
and enter the hallway
of fairies and queens

come stroll through the heather
and open the gates
and enter the cloudy playground
of calm humming
see spirals, feel nothing
build abstract devices
feel caustic rubber balls
bounce off of great stone walls

stay here for a while
a decade, a lifetime
or never return to
the pure maiden's garden
a king in the kingdom
with abstract devices
or cog in the wheel
in a concrete inferno

(1996, *The Village*)

BRITVA

Mother, I hate my body
please put me back where you found me
tired of my shielded mind,
parrot-tongue, mechanic hands
my eyes are full of illusion
fed by the beaks of allegiance
want to jump out of my body
flaunt the blood flow through my veins

protected by my skin's film
want to dig for my second skin
film's always there to protect me
in the end it harms (living this lie)
in my room I shed my skin
coiled, in the absence of others
regenerates all the same
day by day in the presence of others

now I sit in my cocoon
wondering what form to assume
hand me my wooden bible
tell me everything is okay
worms eat and tear off my skin
scream at the sight of my body
masqueraded through it all
no doors can lock out One's Stranger
door crushed – turn to the vices
contemplating deep in sorrow
misfortune loosens the film
learning to befriend the stranger

(1996, *The Village*)

MESSIAH (L.H.O.O.Q. II)

see them march in line
single file by numbers
through the dark-lit alley
lit by gospel-myth

so caught up in finding truths
to timeless questions
when all that is needed
is just common sense

so sped up in process
by our own creations
there's no time to feed our minds
with useful things

death of time is always near
anxiety and fear
seek simple solutions
for over complex problems

thought processes destroyed
no reasoning employed
ignorance is strength
strengthens up one's futile faith

mind-spawned deities
formed to ease the masses
life in the unexplained
comforted by lies

worshipped fabrications
though strong contraries exist
stuck in a blind, closed life
lest we fall apart

satan's bicycle
again it rides
turn off the preaching screens
or suicide

the machine controls the mind
self-induced suicide
obey in trance-like states
no questions asked today
smile never question
smoke-screens to the truth
no one wants to leave
distorted paradise

(1996, *The Village*)

CITADEL

Here, the fascist whores lay opened, beckoning with hollow chastity: forced into the underworld. Endless thinking in shadows in fear of apprehension by police and firing squad. Read in shadows, fear of Firemen and flamethrowers.

The steel Hound bears a cross look, but obeys and snaps its bladed, iron jaws in the name of God-box.

(1996, *The Village*)

BURIAL

a barter – exchange between fire and ice
never existing as one
the short wick is lit now with doors open wide
tension blown into the room
numb as the tongue of a child stung by wasps
needing and wanting no change
this funland exists in a world of its own
hiding the ice from the sun
shouts from the crowd and knives from a smith
bounce off the walls of inside
inside the flowers continue to grow
dry out and die with the sun
weeds grow in darkness and frost lines the floor
well-kept the light out of reach
crystal ball's clouded can't see the inside
only exists on its own
the cries of a dying man fade out of reach
water quickly turns to ice
numb with no movement strapped down to the bed
in bliss with no worries at all
dream of a time when the fire shone bright
flinch with the thought of the pain
escape to your igloo home deep in the cold
assimilate into the bricks
attending the wake of the morning sun
happy to be stone cold dead

(1995, *Perfect World*)

BALLAD OF THE GODS

so, here are the Dark Ages – virgin-white clad
medieval mindsets with electric fineries
the skies are not the same colors tonight
there's a whirlwind of colors violent in its motion
there's a gentle, kind cross in a white-gloved right hand
while a blood-hungry sword's held behind (the left hand)
the skies will not be the same colors come morning
(Aristotle's trespassing through digitized fields)

and here stands a figure – a new age in motion
already a god (though a never-learned human)
pompous he stands, holds a clock in his past
automated and novel his trinkets now flashing
"we are now gods and we worship ourselves,"
(never mind the fact that all life's now Fast-dead)
"we've no need for your monotheist concerns…
cracked open your eggshell –
you've been wrong all along"

today breathes the sky and its mist is of many drabs
indoctrination of those once intolerant
roles have been switched, but fascism still smiles
the Holy Ghost now praised is that of Machine
(but that's all it is – a ghost, nothing real
Arrogance: bashing a ghost of the old
deifying another – a ghost just the same
fools run around with the keys to the city)

an Indian monk stares
at his mall-bought crystal ball
looks at disgust but indifference at the show
"why would one bother at all with illusions?
nothing but abstract cheaply-sold placebos"
he sits as he sits until one day he Returns
if he thinks he'll be back
he's got one thing coming (nothing)
he's wasted his time with his own games

all specters have us leashed up good by the neck

(1997, *Perfect World*)

THE ACTIVE MAN

strawberry-fluff-pillow patch soft and dandelion daze. grab the blades. tear your pants. "how's about a snow cone, kid?" (you offer the child vanilla, but he insists on orange). lie back, the sand holds you in its arms as your eyes roll back – your snow cone's dripping. now, the sandbox is a jungle, and the fertile soil's your making. a win for the cosmic man. your own you own. and you make use of your hands. the stars are very bright tonight, but they look better under your own light, don't they? the porcelain child is intrigued. one day he'd like to grow his own palm trees in the sand. but, for now, we'll have to settle for God's. [i'll make my own offering: i look down – the meat and smoke's my own].

(1997, *Perfect World*)

VIXEN

underneath the tombstone Jesus fumbles with a pistol. Russian roulette, spin the bottle. "how's about best out of three?" He mumbles to Himself and sighs, "the graverobbers have sandpapered my face. it's time to go back home with mummy, and Buddha, and that mental patient from below." like visions in the wind.

she sits reading stories underneath a burnt-out bulb. grabs her scissors, looks for her son. he is sucking on his thumb. the blade comes to a close. a scream. a soft thump pelts, the carpet's been discolored. what a shame. just then on the television: a crown of thorns is drenched in pools of blood. a bullet shell's 'neath a pair of scissors.

cherry roses for my love. silver armor for the dove. we've been locked up in this cardboard box and cannot pop the lid. what you need are glasses. so find your executioner.

dripping from the wax sky, 50,000 creatures gripping pink bananas – it's the Last Meal, as they offer it to him. he grabs his magic crayons. he colors pleasing wallpaper for his room. the sky falls through a hole. back home, she is sitting. her fingers, whom she's loathed, are now gone. and the blade belches. back home... the eructing blade shimmers.

(1997, *Perfect World*)

CORI CELESTI

the old-time Spaniard is afraid and full of fear
for his mighty fortress lies atop a shaky foundation
and we wear his habit and ride forth as today's Spaniards
with his memory dangling in front of our horse

"there is no justice in this here town,"
cries the man tied to the stake, smoke in his eyes,
"there's no point in belief anymore
if it's not loaded in a gun"

there are two ways in which to go:
      the well tread path in the tunnel where the walls
         are lined with braille
         in case the rabble need to move,
      or through valleys and through forests where
         more than plants will grow
but, of course, you'll choose the tunnel
for in the forest there is danger
besides, one's fatigued from looking over one's shoulder,
      or just starts to go insane

and the blood spills everywhere
but in the tunnel of love
the thunder cries in contentment of its global unity
(but at what price? blood for love like death for freedom
      – it's a rip off! rip off! rip off!
      we've been ripped off!)
and it's all done for a Man who wasn't even sure of his
      own identity ("who do you say i am?")
the Man of which the Spaniard who gave us the dangling
      memory supposedly loved with all of his heart and
      stones

what a rip off!

may we choose between the rabble and ourselves (in
 which we can fill up the vessels that we are with the
 mountain stream waters of the forest)
two roads to choose from:
 body and mind,
 stupidity and wisdom,
 racist and heretic,
 light and shadow,
 shadow and light
take your choosing

in the dark tunnel you cannot turn back –
why would you?

a poison cake has been baked
gather around the table
let's see who'll eat it
(have some wine, it's quite bloody)
"eat up or i'll shoot, you hairy desert dogs from hell!
And forget about Ishmael!"

so, the red rivers run
beneath St. Valentine's Day billboards
there's no maybe for the Spaniard –
there's only One
though the Spaniard's dead, his spirit lives on
oh, how it lives on!
unshackle yourselves
and fight the Crown's horse's shadow
bogspeed be with the weak

(1997, *Perfect World*)

WAYWARD SOULS

don't tell me you care. tell me you Care. you may get tossed
by the wind, but…can you really fly? a Stranger's prize ("i
know when my mother died") – he'll still clutch the gun in
his hand. lying there in the vegetable garden with the
cabbage and the blood in the dirt. T.A. reconsidered –
suicide's for clams (as the opera house went up in flames).
drift on by and you might as well get boiled up in stew
(your worthless stench of blood makes me cry like onions.
besides, i'm cold and hungry [and boats are made to sink]).
from the heart of Emptiness and Nothing comes a pioneer
on his horse, but he doesn't understand the Gift.

(1998, *Britvaica Risen*)

HEUTE

<SNIP> mirror soul – glass shards at the point of impact. –frames per second. flicker flicker. run away…forever. heads in a room will forever spin: flicker-spin-flicker…faster and faster. "what did you say?" drilling a hole to Heaven because the crows are dull tonight. transcendental carpenters (their pockets lined with gold). <SPLICE> googoogloogoo. the perforated sheet's bloodstained fate (find me through the opening). love in fragments. three stains of blood. dot dot dot. sturphriKArppet. hate by numbers. Pollack anger: epileptic machine. shudder. Mustarddrippedstrewnpunches. love like a wounded nurse – it *is* necessarily so. a Cyber Messiah injection to uncalm the still sea (nostalgic novelty crumbs neonly decorate a million faces). a falling leaf is dreadful. anxious – very anxious – for presents. trapped in nature. "caw caw!" if no one's here, who is? you're dragged off by a steel horse until you're able to run on your own. run for your lives. run to your hives. a man of tomorrow with a scissorscarred face. multidrabbed iron circle never stops. spilled. so shall you.

(1998, *Britvaica Risen*)

CURSED

there's Doctor Clash with the Third Reich harp players
take poison in through the ear

there's a death in the west
in a graveyard towards the back
the foliage noise blocks its cross

half a billion heard
half a billion sold
nostalgia selling like speed

8000 listen to the trumpets of angels
whose voices are heard through the pull of a string

     red carpet for you from the mouth of the serpent
     hitchhike on the scorpion's tail

     in the desert
     some faint cries by the Bloodshot Cowboys
     guided by Luke the Drifter

     death in the night
     sunset brings new tomorrows
     melts on a new plastic body that glows

     thrown away dreams found by cats in the gutter
     scavenged and lit up for a brand new life

culture transfusion with watered down feedback
plucking gold hair from the lonely paupers

twenty years ago
the painted men of straw
naïve: they tore off the unshaven head

illusions of free will when still part of the game
Johnny cries: "la me fa sol"

bringing in money with crumbs from the trash can
the army's always here to sing you a hymn

(1998, *Britvaica Risen*)

NURSERY APOCALYPSE

we'd often spend the whole day staring at the window with our eyes of magnet. we'd seek for answers in the sky, but all we'd see was the Dark Lady weaving with her many arms (we paradised in a barren desert). my sister was convinced, but i sensed nothing – but one can always be disabled (i supposed). i took you to the City of Ashes where we'd see the children spying from the pyres. if i would hear, this might be illusion – but for now, the tunnel vision inhibits. "Rise up!" roared an infant. ...she was always deaf to the sound of nothing. she would need her head on a stake. i'm swarmed with lollipop kisses and dandelion touches. pacifier penetration from the eyes of rolling thunder. i'm strangled, but can see the black light. though i already knew, i was merely a teacher (my rolling head was used as textbook). i would scrawl of the tipping of the scales by giggly vinegar fumes.

(1998, *Britvaica Risen*)

BRITVAIC IDEAL

there are no serpents in this temple – no sound of hissing, shades of slithers. driven out by discipline (we stand alone in our ideal – we've scratched a circled "A" with nails and toothpicks on the lens of our mind's eye). but, in our sphere, the walls are torn asunder, and new buttresses of hope are erected. our eyes are pierced by arrows from bows and slingshots and we laugh…how we laughed. the gleaming shrine attracts by numbers – who will sit atop this swaying throne (and in my mind, the dream is ending – i know it would never happen. *and the naïve shall recognize their judgment.*)? fear the rubble (a black light shoots through my head) – a quarry is what they want. i stand alone – eyes closed – and expect nothing (i'll even be selfish and lick the wall, in hopes of severing my tongue – "straighten up those spikes!" they'd say). there is no wait. i'm thrown into the ruins.

(1998, *Britvaica Risen*)

BODHISATTVA

we shall steal the sun for ourselves. i've imprisoned Avalokita in my cuckoo clock (feathers combed with semen: "kukukukuku..."). obliterate the senses with year-old candle wax. seven times it's been snuffed out. boring wounds on a Kuroe-Cho hill to fly away with crusted wings (until then, you'll hang like a rusted chocolate warrior with your arms ripped off). a toast to the shining corpse (we've waited for so long). orange cakes for baby – there goes the smokestack.   posed   before   the   people: xylophoneribsmacked. locking Euchrid in a stable with the goats. his flapping skin was ripped off his hands and stuffed down his throat. the children gathered round and laughed because he wore a diaper (they would not listen) – a fish hung from his side by a silk string. [so i shall steal it for my own ("kukukukuku..." they would not listen)]. i'm etched in cheese with lead pipes through my hands and feet.

(1998, *Britvaica Risen*)

ANNIHILATION ZERO

a tree made of seashells lights the top of the hill; you're welcomed to it – a stool awaits you (don't forget the toothpicks). a shortage of gods on a golden dawn. a pile of rotting hands relaxes under a shady tree. wasteland cries from the spiders. we can rent the Resurrection and watch it in slow motion (this will do instead). the sun goes down and a cry has been lifted. where were you yesterday? swapping souls with the king's cattle. faking departure in the Bardo. in the ruins lies a walnut – crack it open if you can. swallow the earth with the shells in your teeth. lost your glasses underwater. where's that smokescreen coming from? upright posture for climbing flagpoles. teething teething. greeting the velcro. swallowing purple. doubting digits. yes. this is the way ("come on in"). more more more. haunting in the zero hour. rockbellyuplift. this is it. stroll through the beach with your hammer and nails...searching... nuclear babies dipped in vinegar for pollen. watching from the plastic trees and flinging grenades. accidental devils from the iron womb. going bankrupt in the cinders. getting sleepy in the ashes.

(1998, *Britvaica Risen*)

AS WE LIE TREMBLING ON THE ICY PARK GRASS

time stands still
and this day *will* last forever –
though this eternal is not the everlasting
      it is often forgotten
      this *is* the eternal –
the clouds cease to flutter
and the trees stand still
and again, the stone is frustratingly pushed up
      the impossible hill

you are always what you are
never what you will become
in this earthed park
the gates are open ("come inside")
yet, there is no leaving
the gates are open and the park is entered

children play by the stream
and…many years later…
still, the children play by the stream
their clothes and playthings tattered with age
balls are bounced with daggers
clutched in opposite hands
the grip is grown tighter
as the ball is maintained in steady bounce

at the bottom of a hill, a piano lies crushed –
tossed from a cliff by resistance met by attempted
        advancement from the secondhand
        on the great clock –
"how dare you change position!" –
though dismantled,
a dagger wielding child continues to play

meanwhile, the heretic's graveyard comes to life –
bones still milkwhite fresh
turn around and see them behind you
there is no change
there is no change here
once again, skulls are crushed with the shovel
the shovel glistens in triumph
underneath a still and saintly night, and…
the gates remain open…

the night lies as still as day
and day is night
and though one tries to stop the spinning wheel
the Princess is gone

the gates are open…

an innocent tortoise is intentionally stumbled upon
sipping water at a now misshapen puddle
"i've said no such things,"
he replies at his given attributes,
and walks away in disgust
curious at such ventriloquisms,
he attempts to walk on water at a nearby pond
        and drowns

the smoke stack signals
and the flag is lowered
a sick man is bled to death by leeches
a wrongly accused woman is drowned in Salem
you wonder how they put out fires here,
as you reach for your lighter
"not yet," i say
"not yet"
the rearview image is used to drive
"BRING ME THAT OLD TIME…"
"not yet"

and:
the leaf falls faster
        than the apple from the tree
streams flow quicker than light
and everyone speaks faster
than the pace of their own thoughts
though the orbit spins faster
it is always noon
all spins in great chaos
spinning and spinning
hear the grind of machines as heartbeats quicken
faster and faster
spinning and spinning
all spins in great chaos

the gates lie open
        while all spins in great chaos

so, here we lie on the steel cool ground
where we talked of setting the trees ablaze
we shall set this whole world on fire
and bring back the tortoise
without the ventriloquists
we shall rust the great gears with our floods
for now it is time
as we wake and grab for our matches…

(1997, *Vinegar Dreams in the Puppet Tree (Video Two)*)

RISE!

on forsaken sparrow wings we'll travel far with candled eyes. our pilgrimage to Mars has proved much useful. Ludi's playing by the lake. the many veins of this new Dawn have sprawled out underneath the moon to guide your hand back home. the goated child with eyes of stone (whose swimming trunks the golden river swallowed) has been captured, and now's singing with canaries. climb inside his punctured hands to see the fate of the running horses, and he'll dance to you the rhythm of the spider. a pile of hands lies on the ground like a cotton ball collection. these hands will never cease to rise up, and will never sink back down. guided lambs fight for position on the switchblade cross (it's tasty and illusion) – disillusioned, they'll know not of sweet nothing.

(1998, *Vinegar Dreams in the Puppet Tree (Video Two)*)

THE SECRET SYMBOL

slipped from the stairs. see how she falls through the sky into raindrops of crystal. at Versailles, in between the mirrors, the teacups are spilling with fruit punch and the dogs are purring like kittens. rise from the puddle and summon the Militia: "looks like we've got a live one here!" stamp a smile upon my forehead and brand my rump with lightning. i'll scratch some code on the bark of a tree (and even out of desperation). bring me Moses with the tablets and i'll show him a thing or two (what i carved into my hand is what i saw and what i'd show you).

(1998, *The Mandorla Device*)

ATOMIC PURPLE

climbing trees and flinging anvils. obtaining enlightenment underneath concussions. from this day forth, we'll sustain injury with confidence. rest assured, we'd have our kingdom amidst palm trees and canaries. wipe those tears of joy; for though i come from nowhere, i am the Immaculate One (perhaps the doctors were wrong as well – they, too, turned their heads up) – take my hand, i'll take you to the forge where i've been brought up since my stay here. by the way, my books are sold here. we'll catch comets by the tail and save our blesséd grapes in an olive jar (we'll leap for stars and even though we'd miss we'd tell the judge that we've gotten more than our share). we must not be condemned. we'll settle for nothing less. bells resonate in red alert: "we'll smash your heads with coconuts if we have to!" the prince is dead, and we'll unscroll the magic spell to bless him kindly – blindly.

(1998, *The Mandorla Device*)

SALT

open and close. the accordion's heaving. one eye's opened, the other one closed. here one second, gone the next (sprinkle sprinkle – where are you?). stars are stars are gods (our gods?). you'll dance for as long as the tune plays. transience is permanent – the man with the plastic armor falls through the sky and is undressed in the vacuum as he's taken back (blink). who'd swoop down to greet us (where are you?)? your predicament is forever hurtful – alone with your wild strawberries. if someone's there, you get no sign ("someone's at the door"). you despise your chore of the Great Nothing. begging for chains – the rattling screech hurts your ears. flagellate from guilt over nothing (you should kiss the stars). thrown on a glass field to collect coins. hammer yourself through a hole. "what's become of…" they ask of me, "…he was here just a minute ago."

(1998, *The Mandorla Device*)

IN BETWEEN A VELVET NOTHING

i saw you falling out of the tree yesterday. you were admiring a threelegged cat. did you see me coming towards you on my modest farm (don't look so surprised...the heavens have always swooped down to greet the rising flames of cities)? my pigs flew towards you as well, and even the chickens would sing. i went fishing in the Amniotic Sea (i remember tugging the lifewormbaited string. your weight cut off the circulation in my finger) and remembered: "Happy Birthday!" you could not know and would not be destined (you'd cook a feast for plastic angels). i feel a tug and sprout out from the flowers to be buried in the mud. i saw the rope...did you see me coming?

(1998, *The Mandorla Device*)

BLACK BOOK

come and peep behind the curtain…Mary holds the child of straw. holding dear this pregnating mudhouse. it is not the harvest of children. weed for the donkey, and leather for pigeons. children wield daggers in search of oblivion…in search of Everything. see their wounds – torched gates to the City. the slithering halo finds its way to your hand ("very good," i commend you) – but, what of the trident? i shall wait for you at the other end of the spiral. when i see you, i pray, destroy me (do not but leave me standing); i'll still see you again. i'll watch you swallow the gods in one breath (again…and again and again…). you'll still be holding the matches and your leather stone pouch. Mary should be holding *you*. we should be cradled. we'll search for the Buddha and give him a dagger (we'll sharpen the blade with Her teeth). he'll rise in the flames, matching his face with ours in the fire.

(1998, *The Mandorla Device*)

THE TEACUP DISGUISE

kiss me with your guillotine lips. leave your mark, dispose of me. you can find me any time. just be sure to drop me a line (or don't). i'll still be here posting up placards for the Linnaeus Bible (i just thought you'd like to know). how i'd like to feel quite certain that i'd be of use to you. i'm feeling pinned beside the wings of stapled butterflies and fallen leaves. i will reach a higher heaven when Ascension Day has come. i'll bring you a silver dish of roses, then we'll watch the stars. but for now, i'll stay here lonely with no lipstick on my face. and i know you'll never find me, so i'll stand here by this well (i know you can't – i've planned it out this way). your codes wash off my skin. i'll watch the two sides on this Crystal Night (from trees), but i'll just laugh.

(1998, *The Mandorla Device*)

BLOOD CAPSULE

down the stairs from Heaven fall the dice. they're always sixes – pulled the rug out from beneath us. yes, we should still sing while we can. we'll rise up, amplify, sing out of key, and shrill our voices for our sweet Video Jesus and Flapjack Mary (how She looks so sweet and very caring – "Mary, won't you marry me?") – She's selling fast! embrace the weeping widow. don't cry for me, for yesterday's fist holds a switchblade today, and Britvaica sleeps underwater in a bed with soiled Atlantis. gelatin and plastic puppies – they're here for you in doses thick enough to annoy you. "la la…" disturbance. wave goodbye (don't look back). i'll meet you in tomorrow's purple.

(1999, *The Mandorla Device*)

THE MISSION OF MERCY

sulfur baths and thorn bush rollers. "you should be thankful for those pins in your fingertips," said the host to the vacuum cleaner salesman. he would take the place of the Devil's mouse in the hamster's wheel for trying to stop time with a bandage ("no sugar pill for you, now…"). he'd be salty as an hourglass. he'd show you good time. one should feel so lucky. roll the dice and dig for rotting corpses in the basement. we've nothing and we're running out [of]…the door. the light bulb in the sky will blind me yet (no more golden pennies for me). searching for Destruction with a compass. climbing crippled ladders to find the nursery. second chance given to those with hatchets. kneeling before switchblade alters. a one-eyed seer will reveal to you that the crumbling path will take you to that special hour (the grapes in his hand never lie).

(1998, *The Morning After…*)

BLACKDIAMONDBLINK

beneath switchblade nights, the meadow piggybackrides a little boy in bloodstained overalls who washes off with the chlorine syrup. he's mixing life and death in cocktail glasses and whispers "God's the antichrist" in sign language. a splish and a splash and the cave's unlocked: "behold! the glimmering black rust flakes…no heaven could imagine such a treat!" splish splash. the pornography faction bullies with marshmallow kisses. a tithe for Path and tit for tat. a Roman blowtorch used to nitpick in the hair of children picking varied flowers with their jellybean claws in the garden of their own creation. the sensual stroking feather dipped in water's dressed with pubic thorns in piercing secret places to deny and reject Life with its prostitute kiss. we all hold hands and feel Love – our hands have all been glued together, and i'm jealous of the rooster with its virgin death. in an instant of hope, my teeth plunge for a toothpick in my shirt pocket. i'll slice and dice the flaky flakes and follow the rooster home.

(1999, *The Morning After…*)

METRONOME

merrily wept the lollipop. i'll stroke your face at 3 o'clock, and like a genie you'd pop out – a million myths ("they had to come from somewhere!" we'd cry out). a sacrifice in blood. they'd slice your crown off with a ruler and then crawl into a hole. a hundred times they would praise mankind from atop their flagpoles – hanging on by swinging tails. and when the scales appear in the sky at 3 o'clock, the scything image will descend and laugh because the calendars were etched in stone. the stones were just mirages. you ate for days and days. the hourglass…it bled and bled (you never knew it could have poured you a drink). merrily broke the fiddle's string. caressed your face at 2 o'clock, and like the dead, i could not sing.

(1999, *The Morning After…*)

VELVET TORTURE

maybe with apocalyptic feathers we will glide up to the turtle's beak and understand the Wounds of Five. she's trapped behind the zebra's flesh. that cage of black and white belongs to her. she's in the library writing books with unseen claws and unimagined tentacles. she'd prescribe while we'd subscribe (though she could never imagine living that creature – *forget about koala fantasies!*). He'd be an egg in Dimension X. she'd scribble herself out of existence (meanwhile, He'd erase Himself into it). somewhere there's a space. somewhere there's a something. on that lonely hill i will mount the cross with my brand new set of unsharpened pencils (i would need no blade). i'd be ripe for lizards, and while she tumbleweeds through empty halls, i'd shake hands with Annihilation. she would not know me now (she could not – nor could she fathom such a concept). even though she'd know, the Question would always be wrong (she would be so lucky) – she'd still be speaking through her webbed feet. for now...i'll wait to melt to sand.

(1998, *The Morning After...*)

PARADOX

halfway to reality. and halfway to again. again and again. never reach the mark. the waltzing candle's flame will never touch me. halfway to ("oh weary feet"), but still a rose is etched in stone. symbols squeezed of liquid gold upon a tombstone where a Zen dog's mouthing "no no no." just like jelly. i crush the numbers in my palm. i'm munching on a cracker. and a flask of poison words is shrined beneath the bed. i sense the smell of oysters, bite my lip, and then stay silent. halfway in the strychnine egg. "hold your tongue, that you may get there," i whisper secretly to my other hand. you leapfrog towards infinity. build your kingdom in the quicksand. if you could touch me, you would know me. i can wait forever, and for now, i'll laugh in silence.

(1999, *The Morning After...*)

PERFECT WORLD

PATRICIDE, NOT GENOCIDE. Serpent Father spins forever. blind Shahadah ("Trust us"), free subscription – "everything will be all right." Holy Father slithering silver tongue. Soldier Prophets made in the Iron House to crush the blasphemers with the stomping boot and the showering of bullets from AK-47s. silence is golden. Father's soothing venom's for our own good say the recruited children. spilling His venom into veins. a blessing in the eyes of the fed: pornographic injection – flowing liquid metal sounds inside once clean bodies. The Purge. "remember the Warring States!" come let father tuck you in. [PATRICIDE, NOT GENOCIDE]. another syringe, another triumph. justification lying in a standing army made legitimate through proof of conviction of tameless wildness of a rabid beast. make room for daddy, the good Lord is here!

(1997, *Video One (1995-1997)*)

HISTORY OF A WORLD

underneath clear, blue skies, your devils of discourse cut
through – trailblazing in black – and cut out my tongue,
while spitting their darkness into my emptied mouth...

the loathsome-voiced strewn air
chokes me in your temple
and hammers me deep
takes away my desires
i flinch as you teach
change children into soldiers
i'm reading your books
i never wanted to die
you tell me: comply so that you'll have a good life –
preserving your spit on the roof of my mouth
perpetuating aphorisms of devils
so you can sit Free in your ivory towers
i'll create my own light – *i'm* God, not your soldier
...

(1997, *Video One (1995-1997)*)

THE MASSEUSE

where have you gone, my friend?
do you still exist?
i'm existing in overt fields
in rain-pissed-on arenas
where is your silent face?
your quiet, statue-like soul
stuck here in the open
in this piss-bloody hole

i sleep with poised microphones
i'm never untouched
my room is full of chopped up hands
that spy in the dark
the silence is a humming screech
conceived by machines
i'm reading in showered fields
i'm left unaltered

turn your life on with a switch
feel electric commands
shift responsibility
to frolic with gift wrap
complain for disquietudes
blaming your gods for your mistakes
land's sprawled with sedated, lazy robots
leashed up like dogs

adults pour through flickering wombs
light shines womb-to-tomb
grow up in their pre-made world
then die as children
guards wait by your front door
blinds pulled to reveal telescreens
hand is still perched on the body
oil poured on to soothe you

(1996, *Video One (1995-1997)*)

THE RED ROOM

Lightning of solitude. Jump on the bolt of loneliness and ride the speed. Traveling faster, off to nowhere. Run from sunlight into darkness, from the cornfields to the cell. Solitary confinement. Once a fruit, now a withered pit. Maggot-driven decrepitude. Gnawed quickly by speed, aging miserably. Cry for tranquilizers – suck the pain. Injecting colors – a placebo found out – nothing but drabs (greys and blacks). A cell for citters to cit in. Where did the bars come from? Fists from smiles (fascists from dogma). The annoyance: all smiles no brains – the shovel which crushes the skull. Look over the shoulder (constantly) in the cell for the traveling smiles. Piercing lips gazing from around the dark corner. Ride the lightning once again. Off to another distance. Running in circles. Running in place. All smiles, no brains. Fists from smiles. Tear out the hair (with it the flesh – red head). Scrape at the eyelids. Where to next? Back to the hole – blood bucket. Down the conveyer belt. Time drags with a chainsaw slicing red rooms. The atmosphere burns holes in skin. Outer skin disintegrating. Flesh rots away. Skin peels away like dried glue. The red glue falls to the floor in sheets. Wallpaper on the carpet. The floor's now the side walls. Sleep on the walls and fall out the window. Fall in the hole, but land back in bed. Sameness. Aching repetition. Death's more interesting at the moment – different stages of decomposition and decay keeps one's interest. The putrid smell is a wonder. …But, NO! – a dry existence. Parched-dry throat. Blistered with aridness. Swallowing blood. Twitching nervously from the lips. Choke in blood. The gazing, eyeless lips. Drown in blood – suffocation. Lips drill holes in soul. Slip on blood, breaking neck. Slip and fall into repetitive nothingness in the red room.

(1996, *Video One (1995-1997)*)

YOU AND I IN OUR OWN SHADOWS

the foul Breath shall reveal the beauty of its essence. it is that which transcends the ephemeral permanence of the Revered One – He with the ring about His head and the rattle upon His end.

> satellites whisper their orbits. their hovers are silent. their motion is but a preconceived plan. rattle these bodies will not. they are only here, and shall always be. there is no Death, only death.

the City of Eleven Gates ("discard of your bones upon entering!") is forever sacred. but...ants from the City of Fire will penetrate. i stand by the gates. i am waiting for you, but come you will not.

i catch a lonesome ant by a fruit tree. the forked tongue threatens me, for i have dreamt of murdering his father. two entrances have already been blocked. my visions of blood leave me with no admittance here. i would like to cut off my hand and flow to the ground so that i may Return. i would soak the wooden doornailed boards into cardboard so that i may tear them off with my bare hand. i waited for you so that i may have your hand as well (i remember once gazing into your mouth...). you had such nice hands. i stand alone as such. the Breath reveals to those who take notice: to those few. ...as such.

a tarp sheet is spread across the city. the body's surface i can now see. i can see you now. you are in the park built by the old man from Kuroe-Cho – he froze to death for us. in the distance, i can see you picking jewels from the mouth of a toad, and place them into a bag. i thought of approaching you...to warn you. you would Fall. i would whisper the secret of Nachiketa into your ear (in desperate vain!). as i decide to call to you, ants start crawling up my leg. i keep walking. i walk as though my announcement would wash away this red sheet like water. i fall to one knee. she did not even flinch.

you had started your second bag.

(1998, *Video Three*)

THE ZERO CRUNCH II

Sheila was a refugee. she'd cha-cha from the tapestries into the nursing bladed mint chips (they'd slice a smile into her hips). swivels to the Esquilax Flux, holds Infinity to her breast, grabs the spanner and the banner with the argent embroidered "9999", and took her leave. she would have nothing of Nothing and stuff her head with pretty flowers. munching wings off evolution (no confusion – mixed solutions). "climb the stairs and go spin through your legs…" is what she'd say, "you'd come up front towards your back, spin the bottle, and then search for the diamond stacks." Sheila was a refugee. she'd cha-cha from the tapestries. oh, how she'd try to whisper numbers swimming underneath swirling skies – i would merely drown in laughter. crashing down – the swaying pillars dive into a sea of carpet underneath the chandeliers where Sheila danced (i haven't heard her count since the end of the world).

(1998, *Video Three*)

THE MANDORLA DEVICE

this day is just another in which hands are dipped into swirling pools of swamp. catch the currents. add to the puzzle. you shall see me in the midst of silver almond clouds. today we'll have another. we'll muzzle the shouts and break the bony fingers of the ones who scrawl out "*Deus vult!*" on foreign sands. we'd help swamis swallow dogs – we'd thrust our fingers down their throats – and reject their desire of buying our bovine enlightenment (we'd compensate with nirvana tablets). every day is death's day and we'll be raised on high forever. the birds chirp "death!" and children too cry. we'll reunite with our long-lost brother (we'd celebrate – pop the Eucharist in our mouths like jellybeans and get drunk on wine). praise and chant: "sweet punishment!" you will see me with my tunic, but you could never join me.

(1998, *Video Three*)

GUTENBERG'S EXTERMINATION

i shrilled an apology. she hates the way my iron limbs are cold upon her skin at night (she'd even sometimes push me to the floor). i often dreamt of trains. we'd have our cottage on the tracks and wait for the 3 o'clock wreck. i often dreamt like that. she's dreaming of her paradise. and i can tell because her pinwheel ears are spinning quickly. and still i'm waiting for the train, though i know the rails are greased. and there's no plug to pull because it's been concised. my daily waste is stored in plastic. my arm's reduced to an abstraction. the puffs of smoke from my cigarette engage in foreplay with those bare ankles of synchronized swimmers. i'd like to be like them. i exist for 42, and i could give it to them as a gift. but they've already too many. and i apologized. she hates it how my skin sticks to her iron leg at night. she'd even throw me out the door.

(1999, *Foxtrot Leviathan*)

ACTIVATE!

i kiss Orfeo's lips and bring the skeletons to life. like Victorian squid ("there in my bed!"). the ink inside my pen will bring joy to the little drummer boy. the children's toys. a murmur on a fetal page. a hand from beneath the casket's lid. just like a kid. God's a castrato and he's turning me on. a radio knob. my hymns have all been blown away. i sing because i need a sister. *Ave Maria.* i pulled my rib out with my teeth. until i give the angels wings, i'll be the whore of Paradise.

(1999, *Foxtrot Leviathan*)

PIANO

baby was a hurricane until he enjoyed sight again. they gave him glasses, tipped their glasses, cheered three times and wished him well on his sentence – on his road to Heaven. and it's transparent. shades of desire. like reaching out for stars beneath a Sistine sky. a Papal vision. pure superstition. you wouldn't want to know. you'd fear what's most desired. you'd get married in Las Vegas if you had to. praise in God with plastic Jesus. baby ate computer chips. he pulled a gargling chicken out of a basket with a rope, smiled, and grabbed a hammer: he'd decided. winter taken as a mistress. it'd snow on the skins of maidens (how they'd be bashful). employment of a limitation. a catalog of placebos. random symbols. random reality. a shot or ten of Paradise. in a bar he'd see them hit the floor (5000 fed). baby stood there with his mallet. *at least we'd be massaged by angels.*

(1999, *Foxtrot Leviathan*)

GUTENBERG'S EJACULATION

her fingers cartwheel over the keys on her lap. and they're dressed in feathers and ribbons, so she knows she's held in high regard. and her mind's like the key that hangs from the tree in the garden, though she's never seen Day One. i want to be just like the branded, paint an "X" over each eyelid ("please my friend, won't you spare some of that extra liquid metal that's lounging on your fingertip?"). i switched my radio to 2030, but all i got was laughing gas from the speakers, and i sat back and dreamt of mother in an imported straw hat... we're walking hand in hand through the wasteland. we're dodging anvils and tripping over the books of the anointed. heaped up like dirt like so many images before us. a halo's handed to a jester. he's jumping up and down with microphones made out of flesh. and would i like to buy my ticket? there is no need. i'm already here.

(1999, *Foxtrot Leviathan*)

LEVIATHAN FOXTROT

we hold the priest in utmost confidence. he'd serve up wafers for merely pennies. he'd even spread the marmalade. me, i'm just a happy little girl with streamers and some cotton candy on my way to happy days...forever! a telephone made of ivory. a phone call to 1651. he blew rose petals out of his mouth. he actually made us think he was talking to us. they'd be greedy with the world. they'd keep it all to themselves. even dauphins got their share. but, in the Hall of Mirrors we'll play tic-tac-toe with avocadoes. play the lead role in the circus. "can we tuck you into bed, Your Majesty?" we'd show them. yes, we'd show them. he buys his tattered rags from Persian merchants, and he speaks to us with golden words. he keeps his watch from a distant. makes sure he's far enough away (Heaven forbade his being in the same room as us). he speaks about you from a distant. spills a drop of blood in the sea. a social buffer. a triple crown. i wear my hood like a dunce cap. my matches light the sky. and on Liberty Day we met for tea. i wore my favorite space suit and ate my biscuit with some tweezers. but even dolphins got their share.

(1999, *Foxtrot Leviathan*)

ZZZIP! (VIDEO ONE)

tonight we'll slide down the perfumed backs of worminfested bananas. our archéd destiny will launch us into the next Creation (we searched for Shiva so that we may be given a golden arrow to pierce the Accordionist with – we'd slip through his navel!). we jiggled through the corpses of dolphins, fingered the decomposition of horses, and swam through boneclad mud. we'd skip a day or two as we'd catapult into the air. our prosthetic hips would flash and twinkle vibratingly as we'd soar beneath migrating vultures. we'll cover up the serpent's sneeze and capture our salinity in an elegant salt shaker. with all the Holy Water locked in our museum's basement, we know we can go on forever.

(1998, *Foxtrot Leviathan*)

VENETIAN VACATION

Nikki sat with eyes wide open
Thinking hard and gazing softly
Planting her tears in the sand
Swore she saw Gibbons before his fall to grace

Picked herself up from the rubble
Carefully sunned herself dry
"Isn't it all so nostalgic?
I think I'll slip this rock into my bra"

Juan, he leans back in his chair
Strokes his chin and states his thesis
Me, I've heard it all before
Like when he once spoke of civil rights

Now he strokes the hair of History
Dives into a golden well
And he's plowing his bulldozer
Over my town just to find a coin or two

CHORUS:
>   Just like our Venetian escape
>   From one's hobby springs a god
>   Taking vitamins with water
>   Helps you to distinguish right from wrong

And the major dreams of pastures
Wonders what it would be like
And he tells us of his sheep dreams
Right before we're led into debate

And with elbows on the table
We produce a golden quilt
Though we're masters of this lost skill
It's basically just a waste of time and means nothing

CHORUS

Nikki sat with eyes wide open
Thinking hard and gazing softly
Went to Italy last summer
Wrote a book, but I wasn't surprised

Juan, he also went there too
Proposed a goal at a big conference
And this time I'm ready for him
Grabbed my rifle from beneath my bed

CHORUS

(2000, *A Miner Stripped*)

ATLANTIS REVISITED

How would you feel today if I left you in the sea?
At the very bottom
All alone with no key
Would you play in the sand?
Or stretch out your hands
Like the way that you did
When you stood like a statue
In my bathroom
With a potato in your palm?

How sweet you looked
with your hands and face pressed to the glass
Sailing towards your destination
Swimming with all the fish
Would you miss me at all?
Or enjoy your new life?
Or shout out loud
Because you couldn't get out?
Then you'd complain
That the slugs round your toes crawl too slowly

How would you feel
if you knew what's happening in your room?
Yes, but there's nothing you can do
About the excavations
There's so much to find out
Cause we must know it all
And I must tell you that
It beats collecting stamps
Or lint from holes
Or philosophies from the east

How would you feel today if I left you in the sea?
Searching for some buried treasure
Just to kill all the time
We now know all your dreams
Though boring some seem
But they've been jotted down
Anyways, just in case...
Wouldn't you know?
We know you better than you

(2000, *A Miner Stripped*)

SPHINX

Deep inside of the cathedral
Stands a man with rolled up bills
And he's thinking that he should have stayed in bed
And the red streets that he walked through
(just last night)
Already miss him
So he grabs his coat and heads out for the door

There's nothing wrong with revenge
If it keeps your home real silent
The unicorn's been spotted on the beach
And the sinners are now winners
And the crippled man is fodder
When you're witnessing the crowning of a frog

Still, please don't let me hold on
To the greatest love of your life
"What if Mussolini wore a dress?"
Your quaint critical conclusions
Are like Cat's games underwater
They're as useless as a big hole in my head

Now the frog, he'd like to thank you
For your attentive attention
No one thought he'd ever make it big
And the body in his closet
Drops his chin with understanding
They'll be happy for some many years to come

Now you're inside the cathedral
You've left town (I heard you talking)
Possession of guilt never felt so good
And you'd had enough amusement for the day
It's not your circus
As you left you gave a postcard to the priest

(2000, *A Miner Stripped*)

HOW THE APPRENTICE'S CONSCIOUSNESS KILLED HIM

he pricked his thumb to test the point. the drop of blood meant go on. he's off to weave with eyes wide open. to beckon with the slightest hint. i'm offering my skull for practice, and he rides in on a slug. i tell him where to shove the needle. have him choose the color thread. purple is for unicorns. red is for a candy cane. yellow's for a night with Lisa. white is for a New Tomorrow…so he threw that one away. and though i feel the tug between my ears, i can still hear the coughing cat. and all i wanted was a kiss from Nero, and he bragged of shaking Pilate's hand. he thought he knew it all like the back of his hand, but there's no room in here for the living. how they'd laugh at the sight of him. he'd be a walking "Pin the Tail on the Donkey" with those banners pinned to his face. they laughed at his obsessions and at his most embarrassing thoughts (i never knew this side of mother). so i finished him off with his very own dreams. and all the while, my eyes were shut.

(1999, *A Miner Stripped*)

PILGRIM

Right from before the start
The gentleman sailed away
He promised the whole universe
He'd digress from disappointment
This is the way we start to sing
Away, map carved in his back
The pilgrim from the sea
Situation's beyond your control
Still you stop for a bite to eat
Situation beyond your concern
But you must have a reason to live
This is the way we smashed his face
As I sat rigid in my chair
I envisioned myself getting lost

Dive into a pool full of lips
They are chattering away their teeth
Although you forgot your bathing suit
It's all right cause they're talking to you
The man stole a country for his name
Now he wants to get into my skull
But I told him never mind
I had changed it just last week
This is the way the body's found
Dirty, but clean just the same
It was hidden beneath my bed
To the house of god you will go
Or to hot dog stands in the east
Many rolls of film to be bought
The pilgrim from the sea

You are racing around the world
On a rocking horse made of veal
And you're convinced that you will win
Cause you gave it enough to eat
Through the ghost town you will ride
Coming back for the seventh time
Hearing voices to reproduce them
He's the pilgrim from the sea
This is the way you read a book
When I heard you talking to her
I knew I did not want to read Rice
And they say that gold falls from your mouth
So I pried in while you were asleep
All I found was a piece of cheese
This is the pilgrim from the sea

This is the way you've tricked yourself
You may run after me and catch me
But you'll never give me that kiss
It gets you through the nights
Especially when fast asleep
I don't understand it at all
So I will not say a thing
This is the way you count your z's
We will steal them until you have none...
Little things amuse me
But this is no little thing
I guess you like what you like
He's the pilgrim from the sea

(2000, *A Miner Stripped*)

BARBARA'S WIKKO

"Excuse me, Madame – where are you going?" You had
rushed off, and I did not have the chance to speak to you.
You were in a hurry, though. Your hands were in the air.
"Miss...are you a butterfly?" I could tell because you wore
the colors. When I heard you smile, I thought I knew what
you'd been up to, but I guess I didn't. "Where are you
going now? I want to know." I wanted to know. I never
did realize why you left me on the swing set. I was left
alone. But I guess you had your matters to attend to. I
never did see you again. "How are you now?" I wondered.
I'd wonder just once more...where did you run to?

(2000, *Man of a Thousand Ecstasies*)

DON JUAN

There we were in the ocean, before our shipwreck. It was me and thirty others. We had not eaten for days, and I had my dog that my father gave me before he passed away. Having not eaten for days, I no longer had my dog. I knew my neighbor who was there too. I didn't know him anymore either. There was a Turk. He liked to handle little girls. He was there too. And, the priest liked his son...or me. The Turk was there too. *Mädchenfresser!* (and *-handler*).

I was the only one left. I was on the beach. A girl took me up and left me in a cave. Her father didn't like me anyways (nor even Zoe). She dressed me up like a Turk too. But I did not get the girl, or Zoe.

(2000, *Man of a Thousand Ecstasies*)

NURSERY RHYME

This place is overfilled with garbage
She's lived like this for far too long
An indication of starvation in the making
The inability to distinguish between fascists and ducks
A vehicle of intellectualism
Babble for a cause, for meaning
The pen – it writes a different story
The goose, now dressed like a princess

It's the language of language
(Bah…bah…)
She's the mother of all saints
From English to Italian
Saint, but mostly not
Hallowed be thy shame
A matter of convenience
If you know what you're saying

CHORUS:
     This is a nursery rhyme

Let's play on the metronome
Let's hear that beat again
Trying to telephone God
1, 2, 3, 4
Did you understand Him?
Did you hear what I said?
There are empty bottles by the bed
Now that you've launched your rocket ship
     <WHOOSH!>

CHORUS

Let's make a reference and make it obscure
Let's pretend we're artists:
"The swashbuckling samurai does not care for Reds"
There…
She's so desperate, she'll resort to anything these days
This is no place for you
A wall between two countries
It's better to speak underwater

CHORUS

(2000, *The Lincoln Caper*)

CALLIOPE

This is what we listen to when we're feeling bored
This is what we listen to when we're living life
Maximizing the distractions with the hymns of peace
Joseph Goebbels
Dominatrix
Love is on the house tonight!

Turn the volume up
Load the syringe to the top
Taking drugs and praying when there's nothing else to do
Totalitarian optimism for the hard of thinking
The Second Coming's answer
to those short attention spans

Legitimizing prostitution with a PhD
Freedom of choice sold by units: art is not for free!
Shouting down the ones
who start the first crack in their egg
Optimism's but a whore that I cannot afford

Rebels shouting in the street, they're looking pretty tough
Room 11, 10 o'clock: we share the same masseuse
This is how it feels to be important: <CHHH...!>
Getting high off noise pollution
Having tea with mom

Agitation setting in ("don't recognize the tune")
Better to resurrect nostalgia again
Fill her up with love: gas station FM666
Beach Boys in the frontlines with their loaded M-16s

This is what we listen to when we're feeling bored
This is what we listen to when we're living life
A grand exhibit selling Meaning like potato pies
So, if you've got no money,
then you'd just as well be dead

(2000, *The Lincoln Caper*)

SHELTERED

"A specter is haunting Europe…"

There's a man of culture sitting there
(Or so everybody thinks so)
And he's full of loaded arguments
That no one has not heard before
And he's just like an artist
With a cigarette in his hand
And he's wet his veins with speed
Because the end of the world is nigh

And he's trying to explain
About the current social structure
Yes, he's an intellectual
And he pays someone to tie his shoes
I can still remember
All the subversive ideas he held
Read it in a textbook
If you like, I'll read it to you in his voice

CHORUS:
> Hail to the death of everything
> Of everything you see

Now we've seen the end of all sense, but
Long live the death of everything
If it's got a title
Or matriculation requirements
I can vouch for it myself
I can't even think of writers' names
Like discomfort from one's grinding teeth
Such habituation's harmful

CHORUS

In the League of Free Thinkers, anyone's an idol…

(2000, *The Lincoln Caper*)

TEDDY BEAR

He's been sleeping with a friend of ours
Been a child since he was young
Transdimensional security
Even his blankets covered his eyes
He slept in this morning
Oh no! Demand is low on Guilt today
And who'll give him his reasons to believe?
Too late to turn to the Hogfather

Sophie was a nurse at a nuthouse
She washed the feet of mental patients
It seemed so strange, but she felt better
So strange, but all her worries left her
Picking carrots in her garden green
Her mother – blown to bits by dynamite
She had to give her body to someone
It seemed so strange when she got married

This is a 12-step program
We got the ad out of a book
We were uneasy cause nobody saw the ad
We left out most of the steps
We killed two cops in cold blood
But our conscience got the better of us
I guess it was a pretty wedding
We also became intellectuals

Raggedy friend will never leave you
It's a tumor in the brain
Sew a button for an eye
He's been a child since he was young
God came to her birthday party
He rode in on a horse
Soon she lost her faith in God
Now the atom bomb makes all her decisions

(2000, *The Lincoln Caper*)

SIMULATION

In this room she stands as the curator
In her Museum of the Useless
And she's living out of convenience
It's always: "Give me more"

And in this town
They're holding boot camp in the market square
Rebel hooligans and mothers alike
Loading rifles with a handful of Jacksons
Better to spend your money than to think

CHORUS:
>I need everything I can have
>Possession runs through my veins
>Oblivious to oblivion
>I think I'm getting bored

A simulation
We're forgetting the next line to the song
A lonesome drifter on the desert plains
And it's coincidental that he's alive
But, not in my town

We're giving it 100%
But only when somebody's looking our way
This is the Lincoln Caper
Assured an insignificant amount
As long as the check clears

CHORUS

I was not alone
I found Nirvana in a dressing room
And there was actually a line
Who says you can't have everything
All hail this right to conquest

The Church of Nothing
Goes to the point of no return
It must be good for something
Jesus has many friends all over the world
It must be nice

CHORUS

(2000, *The Lincoln Caper*)

STORY

Why must we not ignore
That we ignore the fact that
The image we see is only an imagination?
A man once told me these words
I followed him home
He had a camera on his back

It was a game to try
It was a game gone wrong
Someone else told me of playing the mandolin as a drum
An unpure sound from the hands of gods
A stolen tune
But, what of it then?
If I pollute with the eye, draw the gun with your own
Not like a random reflection
Not like he meant it

I saw a face, but it must not have been real
I'll never recover that gaze
And a photo just tells lies
Should I reflect – yes, I'll be sad
(I think I even hear some melancholy music)
Is my stare just a waste?
Only if you look at me
I don't really mean these things
All I want is money

(2000, *The Lincoln Caper*)

KATE'S MYTH

Beaten, forlorn, and slapped in the face
Pushed into the minefield by your guardian angel
Woke up today with a knife in your side
Your future, a coat of bile at the back of your throat
Seems like you should have used up all your tears
Seems like, by now, you'd have lost all your hope
The actor is gone, still the lower depths persist
But at least he'll be going to Heaven this time

CHORUS:
> This is the story, the story of nothing
> You had a notion, but chose not to remember

Cornered, assaulted; like attention by punks
An "M" on your shoulder helps the spies in the city
Looks like you'll be tearing that shirt off your back
I think it was meant for somebody else
That ironed on motto took on its own life
Looks like you will not believe anymore
Still, you'd rather shove those flies off your face
Believing the notion, "Patience is a virtue"

CHORUS

The wind in your hands has put out the flame
But the house has been burning since it was born
Tears on her face, she'd never give up
Burn! Burn! Everything must burn!
Reserving vengeance for just the right time
Gets you nowhere…
Speaking the language with broken meaning
Taking one all the way back to step one

CHORUS

(2000, *The Lincoln Caper*)

DECADE

You act like the stomping boot
You sit there with your spikes and hair
Caressing a cigarette like you caress Ignorance
Even oblivion's got one up on you
And even in this crazy heat
You fail to recognize the big picture
Your fashionable sorrow and papier-mâché fist
Will get you only so far

The tank stomps down the street
It's splashed with rainbow colors
LSD swirls in the washing machine
It spews out "Peace!" while forming gestures with a hand
On the wall a shadow is cast
It's the sign for Spock
And even in your commune
You're still marked like Patrick McGoohan
And in your mind…

And I don't recognize my mother
Because she's shaved her head
She doesn't wear dresses anymore
Casting guilt upon the youth of today
For a history never witnessed
They saw my newborn first
Before I could even tell if it was a girl or a boy

These are the revolutions of today
Che, X, Lilith, Mickey Mouse...
They are the supermarket heroes
Special interest groups with rifles
We've all got our fancies
Someday the dwarves will get you...

(2001, *The Letter Killeth*)

IN THE HOLE

Right outside of the Paradise Inn
Slumps a man tied down to a cactus
Bright and early almost every day
Each new day brings its own flashback

It was Max and Moritz's first trick
I can hear them snickering from here
Keep an eye out for the vengeful widow
This song is the second prank

     Too many buildings
     Too many popstars
     Too many scientists at the foot of their temple

     Too many businessmen
     Too much television
     Too many swimming pools and not enough space

     Too much compassion and not enough sin
     Too many people without tactics for revenge

     Too many artists and not enough money
     Too many Christians and not enough thinking

     In the hole

Too much happiness without the reality
The picture you've made's been painted with blood
Hang your sunset on a wall of flesh
And I'm still thinking of you

I've seen the bottom; I don't like it at all
The light's above us, but it's less than perfect
The hits keep coming, everybody's happy
Happy every day in the hole

Compensation's being served with the drinks
But you never get what you're hoping for
Too proud to stay, you get up and leave
But these days, it's all just the same

Too much defense and not enough of attack
The final joke is coming back in a loop
The grinder's ready, the manual's on the desk
But somehow we forgot how to read

Too many buildings...

(2001, *The Letter Killeth*)

STRANGERS IN BOLIVIA

I saw you at the airport
You were following success
You were sitting with a preacher
Just in case you cast some doubts
And you finally cashed your chips in
After eight long years of work

You are a stranger in Bolivia
You don't have any friends
Just you and all your books
Until the very end
Preparations made for progress
Like a bird singing in a cage: "Hope!"

So you'd like to save the world
But aren't in the mood just yet
And you'd like to write a poem
But you write a check instead
Besides, Monopoly's more fun
In your circle of friends

In a world of pragmatism
Culture's nothing but a hindrance
Ideals kept in isolation
They're placebos anyways
And the poet's executed
And nobody seems to care
Rest In Peace Croniamantal!

We were sitting in our trunk
Having oranges and mist
You gave yourself to God
And me, I just stood there
A philosophy of Nothing
Sounded good at the time

The grains of sand collide
With the impact of an explosion
The chance to live is nigh
But it all goes up in smoke
Everything's a sacrifice to imagination

(2001, *The Letter Killeth*)

RATS

No one saw the coming of the end
Cause their eyes were fixed to what was laid ahead
The blank eyes with skulls and crossbones
And with tumbleweeds for brains
No one heard the silence up ahead

All the monsters have crawled back beneath the bed
There's no more to fear when we have the love song
There's a tombstone in my closet
And I don't know how it got there
I hear they come with each suburban home

It's a simulation of life that's gone wrong
But in these Layouts everything is fine
Delivering eternal life –
What God merely promised
Disorientation's part of Paradise

There are blue pellets being sold for our homes
So our showers can give off an almond scent
And there's poison in the water
But we drink it just the same
Opposition's too much of a chore

And every ideology's the same
Conservatives and anarchists fine tuned
No one can prove that they exist
Work, rest, play, then die
Besides, it's easier to dye your hair
Than to stand up and to die for your beliefs

Sue ended up in an institution
Because she always rambled like a child
Institutions of society
Avoid them: the more the better
Education's not the real way out
I guess I'm destined to live with the rats...

(2001, *The Letter Killeth*)

A DAY IN SPAIN

Here is a man who wants to meet us
He is a lower-class elitist
The one they call The Man has got the brains, they say
See him tied up

All of the world is in a shelter
Russian Roulette decides the protest
A revolution following the rules of play
So what's the point?

Here come the dwarves…

You are the one who swings the feather
In hopes of making something better
A six-month contract or until the flame has died
Wanda holds her whip

And in your mind, you are sedated
And everybody has been wasted
As long as all the diamonds fall into your lap
What else is there?

Here come the dwarves…

(2001, *The Letter Killeth*)

WAITING FOR THE RESURRECTION

Cold turkey
The occasional desire for gullibility
To believe in the lies and stories
That allow so many to fall back on
But, the yellow spider on the windshield
Points out: "Never!"
And though I understand
It's like the spider's inside me
Gnawing on my intestines
Chewing on my fat
And from these wounds I secrete the pus
Yellow, like the spider itself
(Or so I'd like to think)
At least not now anyways
The dangling of the mocking limbs
Has reduced me to this
It's not God on the window
Like in that old Swedish film
It's something else

From the cross, the drooping limbs
Lifeless and empty
"Caw caw," laughs the crow
Under the shadow on the hill
I'm still waiting for the punchline
Many will be disappointed
In the distant
All I see's a mushroom cloud
This must be the joke
Look!
See how much damage can be done
In a five-minute conversation
The horizon goes pale
It's whole past, flashed before it's very own eyes
Though all we saw was lightning
And all we heard was thunder
And I'm also pretty sure
Though it was hard for me to see
That every other color of the spectrum
Including those unimagined
Was summoned at this very moment
When the past came into the light

I'm waiting for the resurrection
But, I'm not that ignorant
This is not a fable anymore
It's a black book charred
Time is what you make it
And so far, I've made it despise me
The shadow of the mocking, yellow star
Constantly above my head
Just give me some of that old-time opium
Because there are no promises to be made now
The spinning star
Never
The bouncing star
Never
That's all I get for now
The soundtrack of my vigil
The Muzak in the Bardo
Three dead days
And the fourth...
Pitiful, drooping limbs
The painful face of the stoic
But not like in all those paintings
How many more days
Of watching these decomposing hands?
Of rotting away?
Of going away?

But I can wait a week
For a second-rate god
It's all the same, anyways
Or is this an expression of anxiety?

The corpse turns to dust
And a silver ring falls to the earth
I bend to pick it up
And on it
Finely etched
The portrait of a god
But, down below
Is that the halo?
Or is it merely a blemish?

(2001, *In the Animal Garden*)

GUN

Rehabilitation admission form number C33097-8301D
Patient appears to be sleeping
Amidst Korean acrylic tiger blankets
And a wall with an airplane motif
That sometimes makes for sufficient company
Or is it like a girl leered at by athletes?

The click of time
Shoulder to shoulder
Alternating on the bed
In the middle of the night
Making sure the other's not jealous
Pow!

Outside the window,
A car driving by
Bang!
The ceaseless song of the telephone
Pow!
The shuffling of feet
Pow pow pow!

Patient appears to be sleeping
Caving in
A shot in the dark
Nerves like nylon, not like steel
A state that would break Tetsuo
UuurRhHhhh
rrrrrrr...

Poetry of withdrawals
rrrrrrr…
Thought and the muse
Pow!
Curiosity
Bang bang!
A Mussorgsky record in a distant home
Plays Pictures at an Execution to Canadian country music
S T A T I C
Corn on the cob
A lost connection
Pow pow pow!
Shock treatment of the severest degree
Que sera, sera
Maximum distraction = temporary mental invulnerability
<click> <click>
Sleep
Ende gut, alles gut

(2001, *In the Animal Garden*)

FLY ON A STRING

Dangling from a chord
Swung like a pendulum in the wind
Today, the string was clipped from the finger
Gliding to and fro across space
Back and forth
String and all
Because I know not which way to go
You are in the harbor
You are expressionless
I'm carried towards a flickering candle
But try to struggle back
Stuck between two magnets
Hopeless, fluttering wings
A frantic dance with no control
To and fro
String and all
Before I knew my place in the wind
It's August, yet it's cold
Before I knew my place
I was a fly on a string

(2001, *In the Animal Garden*)

I REMEMBER NOTHING

These are the bony clumps
Lopped off onto the floor of this room
Because the wall has nothing more to say
Almost five if you count the thumb
One for every year gone by
Bending down
The other hand picks up the pieces
Of the broken left
Rolling away from the blade
Like the minutes
And I try to imagine

Looking over the shoulder
The anxious haste
The weakness of a spy
Memory is what you make it
Turn around now
A monolith of nothing
A great cloud of sugar
A sugar pill of consciousness
The white sheet over the eyes
Mist inside the turtle's shell
And I try to imagine

The extent of imagination
Taken only so far
Like a yo-yo that never touches the ground
You're lying on the street
I touch, but cannot feel
Gaze, but cannot see
You're a blur that does not even move
As if cut out from a picture
Still squinting, I can't manage
Once so familiar
The missing teeth
The loneliness of forced amnesia
And though I try to imagine
I remember nothing

(2001, *In the Animal Garden*)

PREGNANT CITY, SMILING

This is the sound of nothing kinder
This is the sound of pumping veins
Kites never come back
Trees always burn down
This is the point in which thought starts

No one will dance here
Nobody drinks here
This ain't the pub of pragmatism
Everyone holds hands
Rich kids will form bands
Let's glue our lips so we won't speak…

So it's easier to sleep

(2002, *Postcards from Oblivion*)

KINGS AND QUEENS

Spying from the crenellation
Windows for those roving eyes
Teasing with ribbons of lace
A strong foothold above the rest

A glass of wine nailed to their hands
Working like an abacus
Numbers swimming in those eyes
No time for a velvet glove

> When the hand becomes the rifle
> When the whip becomes a lash
> When the Sirens beckon you
> They always shove your head beneath the sea

You always keep your gold in your closet
But never take it out at night
Those powdered hands of your neighbors
They always put up a good fight

Hands always opened
Never with open arms
Crown hidden in the pocket
Always jangling with jewels

> When the hand becomes the rifle...

CHORUS:

> Hark! Here come the Kings of Nothing
> Place your knee upon the grass
> Curtsy in their mighty presence
> Spread the roses before them
>
> Bow down to the Kings of Nothing
> Kiss their feet and kiss their wives
> A watchful eye upon their children
> But, who says they don't eat their sons?

The lining of the coat conceals the blade
The soft, paternal touch of disgust for the dogs
Is scrubbed and washed
Lest one catches disease

Bathing in streams of gold
The glutton buys his way to Heaven
Looking for the one called Jesus
Can you spare a dime?

> When the hand becomes the rifle...

CHORUS

(2002, *Postcards from Oblivion*)

BROKEN CROSS

They said you got a broken jaw
On your way back home from church
It must have been a shock to you
When it wasn't on the news
And all the children on the street
Doing all that they do best
Laughed as they had watched you fall
And they called you so naïve

Coffee stains and cigarettes
Chalk dust all over your hands
Trying to crack the laws of space
Before the waiting firing squad
And on that single rare morning
When the sun had failed to rise
Your life had flashed before your eyes
As the rifles pointed to you

And no, you will never again believe
No, you will never again believe

> And all of the stations of the mind
> They are never what you expect
> The finger paints will blend together
> Away with Disney, Einstein,
> the Iceman, Jesus, and Plato

And now you're sitting in your room
On the floor with the bottle
Marbles sprawled in a circle
The bottle spins in the middle
And when you're waiting for the outcome
You will keep your fingers crossed
And I'll bet money against you
When the bottle points to you

>And no, you will never again believe
>No, you will never again believe
>And oh, will you ever again believe?
>No, you will never again believe

(2002, *Postcards from Oblivion*)

BUZZ

Here comes the modern man!
You're waking up to find yourself
In the same exact place
In places where you've never been
With people that you've never seen
It's fine if you're not up to speed
It's all about commodity

This world we own's of cottage cheese
Or so it seems
The scheme of universal love
Conspiracy! Conspiracy!
It's all about the words we say
And throwing out the cultural glitch
Saying it with dollar signs
And matching up economies

The decentralization scheme
"I want a piece!"
The beauty of life's differences
Converging towards a great, black hole
Coppers, fuckers, Christians, bums…
Even cats all look the same
So what's the use of language now?
Here's a random word for you:
      KNIFE!

This night will never turn to day
As long as we have lies to say
A cactus with no prickly thorns
A pirate with no wooden leg
C.c.'s making lemonade
The children with the needle play
The litter box is filling up
With arms and legs of other men

Here comes the modern man!
You're waking up to find yourself
In the same hospital bed
The window's closed
The curtain drawn
The book is out there on the lawn
The nurse comes in with eyes like yours
A smile like yours
The switchblade drawn

GASHGASHGASHGASH!!!

(2002, *Postcards from Oblivion*)

THIRD TIME FROM THE CELLULOID

Beware!
For the flapping of the mosquito's wings
Prevents you from clear thought
Consciousness may not come easy
But it is he who knows
Yes, it is he who knows

Do not stand in its shadows
Do not stand beneath the tree
That self-same tree
Yes, the one that the Buddha hides in
And stares down upon you with envy
He's as clear as crystal now
And he can be seen through
The earth shivers at this revelation
But, will you stand as still as the tree he hid in?
Will you stand so still?

Do you recognize the shrine?
Four turtles climb upon the rocks
The candles flash an Indian temple
Upon the wall
Upon the wall
A ziggurat of knowledge
A lie that has taken the form of the previous line
For common sense is esoteric
And it is known
That all monks are ghosts

The bees mate in my ear
And the wasp steals me some honey
A hallucination into a greater world
Reveals that which is feared
And in the jungle of posterity
Nobody's a winner
Because nobody is playing
Yet, the merchants still give advice
Free of charge or not
They're still written down in books
And are gazed upon
But it never goes beyond that
No, it never goes beyond that

A knock on the door
The feedback is looped
Four fingers crawl in through the crack
Through the crack
What is this message?
That which we seek
The gods are in the brothel
Because they know…
Because they know

And will you take this with some salt?
Or will you hoard it all in cupfuls?
Will you take it?
Will you take it
That you are merely but a grain of salt?
A single flaw in a concerto
A blemish on a painting
A sign of life upon a blank stare
A single grain of salt
A single grain of salt

(2002, *Postcards from Oblivion*)

SABETH

Look to the past
These memories
An anchor lost at sea
Your face is sewn into
The blanket of oblivion once more

The children with your smile
Strapped to the barbed wire linked fence
With eyes like yours, but
With strips of torn skin flapping in the wind

Where is your face?
The blade of a knife
Sharpened in the mud
You're photogenic
Can I slip my life into your skull?

Here in my bed
The heat and insects visit me at night
The image branded
Deep inside the callus of my mind

Out by the sea
Matchstick soldiers singing in the rain
Their heads are striking rocks
Nostalgia: Her sparks will never glow

Ribbons of lace
The objects that attach you to the post
The images you see
Will knock the chair over beneath your feet

There is no place for regression
This is no place for the broken steps of man

(2002, *Postcards from Oblivion*)

UNDERWATER SUBWAY

Knock the tin can on the wall
Knock it on that concrete wall
The little black-haired children lost
Lost as to how to respond
A young girl in the corner drops her chin
Her eyelids hiding her expression

The rhythmic beat of tanks rolls by
Doppler Effect in full regalia
As it shoots its ammunition
To the crowd of aging Catholic widows
It's a lesson in realism
Or so say the tin hat martyrs

CHORUS:
    Underwater subway scheme
    Nothing's sacred, but obscene
    Underwater subway scheme
    Underwater...
    Keeps you in the dark

A family down south on the streets
Their friendly singing's being looped backwards
It's all part of technology
If it's tangible, it's feasible
As concrete as the wall
We can touch it, we can feel it

This is what it's like to live
A cobblestone road right beneath your feet
Away with Lhasa, and away with Eden
We've got your apple wrapped in cellophane
We've made a log of all your guilt
And we have kept your prayers to prove it

CHORUS

The stars are imploding into nothing
In the night, the dreams all end
No more white light, no more white noise
No more imagination
It's all downhill from here
Until the cherry bomb cushions our fall

And yet again, the submarine
Underwater – so extreme
The loop restarts, but we don't mind
The cactus pricks will now retract
The scorpion has lost its sting
A child grown out of innocence

(2002, *Postcards from Oblivion*)

CONTRACT

Well, we rode out the next day... Off to meet our destiny, like everyone else did. Like others will. Up the scoliosis hill. To shake hands with God.

His body moved in a serpentine motion. He wore a green bow. He handed us green pens with which to sign our contract. Others would follow. Nobody would be left out.

So, this is capitalism. It begins with this contract. A love for accumulation. A trance and a drug. The Ferris wheel in our eyes would never stop. Not for you, nor for me. A hypnosis initiated at conception. Monopolized before birth. Green is the amniotic fluid. Green is the sea. The feathers, the room, and the penknife... Well, you get the picture.

(2002, *Postcards from Oblivion*)

ART CLUB

So much talent
Under this roof
So much talent
Under one roof

CHORUS:
>   It's amazing
>   When one thinks of
>   How much growth
>   May sprout from this seed

Devotees of vision,
Mind, and inspiration
Intellectualism
The next Don Quixote

So long, Picasso
So long, the laymen
This circle of comrades
Can only get smaller

CHORUS

So very amazing
It's all so profound
When the public
Admires these works

So much talent
Under this roof
But, even pineapples
Are destined to rot

CHORUS

So much talent
Under one roof
Provided it's not set
Aflame in the night

(2003, *Like Pineapples in a Hothouse*)

CINDER

You are nothing
A black pile of ashes
Set from within
You're a human candle
I stare at your feet and take in the lingering vapor
There's nothing in the room and nothing upstairs
Matching denseness sprouts
from the heap of your remains
Taints the soil you walk and others who follow
You feed the machine
It acts as your lover
Coquettishly it laughs
It wants no other kind
It feeds you matches under a watery sky
I wish I could ignite everybody else like you

Always nothing
You stuff your face with deceit
You eat off the plate in shadow of two-faced coins
Feeding your clay figure
So easily moldable
You start to sense the sparks
You quickly want to change sides
Your hair starts burning right up from the roots
Your crystal head is next
I always saw through you
An uneasiness begins in your knees
As a smile emerges on our faces
And you fall to the earth in a pulp
I want to see you go down with a flame

(1995, *Like Pineapples in a Hothouse*)

TZAK TZAK

"Meet me at the station," was what she said before everything in her life came crashing down upon her. She was a victim of ideas. She was a monument to herself, which in itself was created by bricks and stones held together by nothing else than more ideas. "Quickly now…" You'd miss the train. Stumble through those streets of Europe. Pick up matches along the way. Points of interest lead to sparks. Another good idea along the way. Shake hands with the corpse. Another good idea. Yes: an irregular pulse. Head weighs a ton.

The chocolate-brown coat with the feathery trimming flutters in the distance. She's a speckle up ahead. She's a spot on the horizon. Catch her with binoculars. We know that there are bandits. And time will sabotage the future. The dartboard hangs upon your back. A bull's eye in the dark. A good shot in the back. My best friend holds the darts. My favorite enemy holds the cards.

"Hurry up, you'll miss the train." Stepping over curbs. Sidestepping over selfish minutes. Whisking by the addicts with the blue horse in the tunnel. Skipping stones and skipping rhymes. Up ahead: a flagpole in the ground. Say your farewells quickly, and then run. Go go go go go…

The chocolate-brown coat flutters in the distance. Time has sabotaged the future. My best friend holds the darts, and my favorite enemy holds the cards.

(2003, *Like Pineapples in a Hothouse*)

ZERO ZERO IN THE YELLOW-STAINED AMPHIBIOUS BOTTLE OF POACHED PERCEPTION, OR 9 O'CLOCK P.M.

The round and round
The round and round
It was a long time, no
It was a long time?
No!
But, over too soon
But it all depends
On which end of the gun you're standing on
Behind
Oder?
Behind

Behind the feedbacklife
Life as a bad habit
A knife in the dark
Your voice
No depth, no substance
'Tis merely objective
An observation of the physical qualities of a sound wave
Clearly, the essence of secondhand perception
The byproduct of cause
The essence of two-dimensionality

Perception flawed
A piece of paper torn in half
Milk, sandpaper, and snow
All blended together in a great black pot
In my ear
And dubbed
Mixed down with effects
Did it have to be black?

You had called me on this particular plane
Apologies for Inconvenience
Reception as null
Revelation in the Null Null
Of substance
A moment *im Klo*
Of mind
A moment in infinity
In the third, in the Next
Two seconds later
See you tomorrow
Don't want to miss you
Lach kanosch
Don't know – to hear you
Lach kanosch
Sketchy sketchy
Lachkanoschlachkanoschlachkanosch
Lachkanoschlachkanoschlachkanosch

(2003, *A Sense of Urgency*)

GOOD NIGHT

A face in the sand brushed away by the hand
Our memory, gone with the wind
We know nothing, and never will
We never choose to dig our own graves

Take pleasure in sin before it's too late
For tomorrow it will be too late
You will disappear like a fading smile
And will be re-cast like the toss of the die

CHORUS:
    We held on to the rail
    till our knuckles turned white
    And waited for morning to come
    Towards the horizon, we never looked back
    The last toast, the last dance
    Good night

CHORUS

The howl of the wind never leaves a trace
We always choose to live as someone
Companion to none, or a knife in the back
Passively waiting for the right time to come

Take pleasure in sin before it's too late
We know tomorrow will be too late
All is in vain; your prayers mean nothing
The last toast, the last dance
This is good night

CHORUS

The last toast, the last dance
Good night

The last toast, the last dance
Good night

The last toast, the last dance
This is good night

(2002, *A Sense of Urgency*)

SOVIET KÖLPONY

Last night the sky changed colors again
The ever-shifting horizon <undulating>
A light switch
Memory explodes
The nocturnal shards that introduce morning…
Like crayons of wax

The bubbles rise up from the lips (<fzz! fzzz!>)
And every night
From each ear, eye, and curious cavity
Colors of all shapes and sizes
Past and Simple Past
Never to be reckoned with
Always to be scrubbed and cleaned
A clean slate
Editors and publishers…
It's the history of the world

(2002, *A Sense of Urgency*)

HEISTERBUSCH 14

When you move
The saw plays in the background
Every movement
A Dutch inflection
Each attempt at rest
Punches a hole in your dimension
It is the third
But, do we share it?

A windmill crucifixion
A line of ducks to cross the street
In single file
With iron boots
Try to sew your eyes shut
No voyage to Mars will render you blind
And gluttony's a virtue
And recognition never pays

In search of fine cathedrals
Christ's message on a postcard
Paper dolls lay empty in a tunnel
The needle passed, the blue light flickers
Glance at the reflection before you
A pile of vomit
The lady of the lake
The dew upon the horse's hooves

Throw potatoes into caves
All familiar corpses lie within
Watering the plants and flowers
The blooming skulls, the photographs
Death is photogenic, dear
Babbles in a foreign tongue
Language as exquisite corpse
The skin inside the closet hangs

(2002, *A Sense of Urgency*)

THE MARAUDING BAND
OF CUT-THROATS

THE MARAUDING BAND
OF CUT-THROATS

RELEASES

Pretty Songs to Smother Your Ugly Babies To (2003)

Tales from the Sea (2004)

UNDERGROUND LULLABY

The possessors of gold
The extractors of souls
A nine to five cancer
It's the right to be secure
The right to a routine
The grind of a routine

This is how we die…

Love is for the weak
Love's for everybody
A wedding in a chapel
A marriage in a gas chamber
Load the canon with the baby
Life as function over form

This is how we die…

Father Jesus in my pocket
The winter light will fall from Heaven
Hallelujah! Hallelujah!
Here's someone else to make decisions
Death with doubt, it's His ultimate suffering
But we still bother all the same

This is how we die…

Learning to read in a bunker with no light
Learning to speak, but never to weed
The sheep-skinned prisoners are marching in line
To pledges and to haunting school bell anthems
And the intellectuals
Oh, how much more they are fooled

This is how we die…

You never talk, you never think
You never mention the social system
The troll under the bridge that will never die
The sin machine – if you're into that
Autonomy failed
And onwards towards Britvaica!

This is how we die
This is how we die

This is how you die…
This is how you'll die

(2002, *Pretty Songs to Smother Your Ugly Babies To*)

SAFE WAYS

The belt's tied around your mouth
All the curtains have been drawn
All those thoughts you had of leaving
Left you behind on the train
And the note upon the table
Nothing's written, but it's signed:
"From the Warden of Society:
Welcome back, let's join the feast!"

There's a book upon the table
And it's wrapped inside a flag
Gagged with wrapping tape
Like the hands around your neck
All the flowers in the garden
And the face upon the moon
They don't mean a single thing
When we come to join the feast

There's marriage and there's love
And a soldier earns his medals
And the only way out that he thought
Was through education
There's a church full of castrati
Aristotle sits in prison
Everyone will hold hands and start singing
When we hold the feast

The belt's tied around your mouth
All the curtains have been drawn
All those thoughts you had of leaving
Left you behind on the train
And the note upon the table
Nothing's written, but it's signed
There's always room for one more body
When you join the feast

(2002, *Pretty Songs to Smother Your Ugly Babies To*)

STRAWBERRY RIFLE (REFLEX)

Tonight, the stars will fall onto the backyard of our mind. The bells will chime, and all the people's prayers will turn to dust. There's only compromise, where once there was hope. And all the cripples will fall. The scarecrows jump out from the bushes like a pop-up book and put the rope to your head. And all those idiots with flasks and flowers in their hair... The drunken bastards drink the wine and all the smiles come out. There's only happiness. The ashtray cradles truth. And only ashes remain. The angels in the trashcan, recycled for hand-me-downs. And all the haloes are mine.

(2002, *Pretty Songs to Smother Your Ugly Babies To*)

SANITARIUM

The fruit falls from the tree onto the ground
These notes we found were buried in the mud
The fossils hold the secret of perception
And the only limitation is the one of our existence

Three physicists and the corpses of three nurses
In the room Newton and Einstein wield revolvers
Rationalism hanging by a string
Like the sinking of a dead weight
Like the noose around a neck

The eyes of the magician fall onto the desk
A sacred language spoken
And the man is turned to dust
Sweet Analysis you are my only one
Dig a hole into my body
Plant your eyes into my skull

Pinwheels spinning deep inside a darkened cave
And a little girl is lost because she uttered her first word
Pull the rug out from beneath her
Semaphores are planted
Now there's a twinkle in her eye

The pen is out of ink, but keeps on scribbling
In the closet hang the limbs we didn't need
Staring into eyepieces with butcher knives
The suicide of mystery
Of spontaneity

The sacrificial lambs are on the table
And you give a toast right before the cops barge in
They're going to put you in a cell by morning
But anxiety became the law
Because the morning never came

(2002, *Pretty Songs to Smother Your Ugly Babies To*)

TALES FROM THE SEA

Once someone has realized one's own mortality
They think they're okay
But, oh…
Have they thought about the flip side?

CHORUS:
>This is how it is
>When you're under the sea
>This is how it is
>In our little submarine

A blind man cowers at his first sight of light
Beneath his feet, the pothole widens
"Come in, come in," it says hungrily
"Come on in for a good time!"

CHORUS

Bob's dumped off at the side of the road
Left as he came
With both eyes closed
Against his will
An accident that's best forgotten

CHORUS

(2003, "Tales from the Sea")

T.O.E.

T.O.E.

RELEASES

Autonomy or Bust (2003)

It's Time to Start Slitting Throats (Live at Scolari's, 2003)

GREEK TRAGEDY

The ivy clings onto the wall
A man cowers alone in fright
A flight to Guatemala fails
Coincidence destroys a world view
What is the point of planning?
Or of believing in fate?
As the vultures swoop down
Nobody will know what progress will bring

If it wasn't for the flight
The turbines would have not kissed God
The angels would have stayed in bed
And the hanged man would never swing
All of the calculations
And the statistical crunch
There's no such thing as believing
For I am Faber: Man, the maker

CHORUS:
    Nobody will ever know
    Nobody should ever know

The winged man from the Atlantic
The brother of the swinging man
I met my daughter on a boat
And saw a snake take her away
Of all the luck in Athens
The hospital – it's off limits
Stubborn, he left from Paris
Ruined the life of two

CHORUS

(2002, *Autonomy or Bust*)

A.N.S.

A.N.S.

RELEASES

The Wickertank E.P. (2006)

OCEAN SONG

Thinking of you
I want to see the seaweed dance
A secret show for one
Want to hear those sounds
Those whispered words that I won't know
But there are cartoons in my head
And ropes of plastics noodles
Have me tied down to the chair
To where I can't do a thing
To where you can't do a thing

Sleeping till noon
I want to hear your creeping steps
And not just in my head
While on the other side
I want to see the mainland strike
I want to see a war
So that it may drive you near
But the birds drop from the sky
And there's nothing we can do
No, there's nothing we can do

Thinking of you
There are cartoons inside my head
How I wish there'd be a war
But I guess I'm being selfish
I guess I'm just that way
And the only thing that's getting in the way is everything
Making it to where I can't do a thing
To where you can't do a thing

(2005, *The Wickertank E.P.*)

WHEN ALL IS SAID AND DONE AT THE END OF THE NIGHT

Strong like poison, as sure as death
Sleep comes only twice a week
Strong like poison, as sure as death
Reaching out in the night, never grab a thing
And the cold night air wraps tight around your skin
Like a leather glove or tender kiss
Standing by the window, waiting for a sign
Everybody's frightened day by day

Brushing off the stranger in the night
That which you don't know will eat your mind
It's a man's best friend, or so I've heard
But one couldn't tell from the expression on your face

Strong like poison, as sure as death
Getting in the way of your experience
Getting by on only good enough
Everybody's frightened day by day
Learn to sing the hymns of nostalgia
Never mind the fact that there is more
Learning to embrace what you don't know
Your very own trip into the end of the night

Mother, mother…hold me tight
Sing me songs that everybody knows
I can't shake this strong feeling of fear
Hold me till the end of the night

(2004, *The Wickertank E.P.*)

KOKESHI DOLL

Armistice
All the money's gone
Let's talk things through
Like the red bricks
waiting in the wall for the hoisted rag –
It's demolition time!
Should we sit around, or should we strike?
I look, and they perceive

> They desire all the movements
> Of a man seen running down the street
> Turn the corner – hesitate
> What's beyond the sea?

Riding on an anchor with a spoon inside your shoe
Just in case you change your mind
K-girl on a bench
She always takes one by surprise:
Everything will turn out fine
Always happy – happy people!
Grab your spoon and go
The time has come
Pack your skin inside a suitcase
The man comes round again

> He desires all the clarity
> Of a man strolling down the street
> Turn the corner – hesitate
> What's beyond the sea?

Xylophone: exposed rib cage tune
Played by beaks of bluebirds
The man comes round again:

> *Efficiently, doubt and the infection of patience*
> *welcome me with open arms.*

(2004, *The Wickertank E.P.*)

PARANOIA MAN IN A HOUSE OF SCUM

I've created a new image of you today
The active hands inside my skull
sculpt a new hated figure of clay
A hated face
Though in the corner
The disembodied voices speak –
     an actual, physical manifestation of reality
Struggling with this effigy –
Tied to a tree and set on fire!

About 1700 miles,
Four hours
Whether measured in time or in space
Distance is the catalyst for imagination
The thin line between reality and imagination is blurred
Wired by adrenaline
<pitter-patter-pitter-patter>
This mind runs wild…

The skin melts off your face
The eyes inside your skull are different than before
Always running to the hole that's yelled into
But the lungs are filled with sand
And so the body just swells up
And sleep ain't cheap
And the bottle doesn't do a fucking thing
The axis of confrontation must have been disoriented
Somewhere down the line...
Now I lay me down to sleep
Everything will be all right
But still, will I be had?
Will the fool stand in the corner
With his head hung down in shame?
With his head between his knees
Should've gone with your first instinct
You should've been a man
A cop with his stick
Look over your shoulder
You should've been a man
And always sleep with one eye open...

(2005, *The Wickertank E.P.*)

RAYGUN CIRCUS

RAYGUN CIRCUS

RELEASES

Under Judas Skies (2014)

Raygun Circus (2014)

Holograms (2015)

Prisoners / Into the Black (2016)

Into the Black (2017)

DNA Parade / Terminal Fiction (2017)

Swiftly into the Night (2018)

The Treachery of Truth (2018)

OH, LUSITANIA!

On the bridge connecting west and east
Face to face with brutality
They've wiped out all the parks
To put up another shopping mall
Half price off and special offers
Excessive force is guaranteed
The red and white
The media blackout
See the skies lit up in flames
But the dominatrix weather girl
Tells us of clear skies ahead
And now we've got Miss Turkey and
The strangest cat of the world

Bruce Campbell fell to Earth
Into the streets of downtown Los Angeles
Dusted himself off and rubbed his eyes
"Welcome home!"
But lost in the world
Checked himself into a Holiday Inn
And turned on the TV
No Book of the Dead
But the Good Book's by the bed
And that cheerful dominatrix
Has got a heavy boot to her neck
So what you see is what you'll get from
The handmaiden of the rich

Cut and stitch
Delete, ignore
Another Frankenstein delivered to your door
Something to say
But this life is not the time or the place

Hush now baby, don't you cry
These walls are paper thin
Lights out
Slip under the wire
And keep your voices down
We have nothing to envy in this world
Let's live our own way
Dead to the world and dying inside it
And so, another day goes by
But join us in the park today
For the children's military parade
Complete with cartoon ducks and tanks
For everybody to see

(2013, *Under Judas Skies*)

LAST CALL

Death of a Ladies' Man blew my mind
But I didn't know in which direction the pieces flew
Thinking about the expanding universe humbled me
A neon sign flashed "Insignificance"
We are nothing
If you're at that far end and I catch your glimpse
I'd be looking into your past
We wouldn't exist in time and space together
But I'm going to drink more whiskey than
The man who drank more whiskey than Brendan Behan
Before becoming nothing
Until becoming nothing

If I were 27,
I'd sing about how I'd been alive for that many years
Arranging my life into packets
that won't be opened until I die
I'd sing about that the way some singers have
But I missed my chance
When you got back to your roots
A line came to me:
There's a sucker born every minute
And this proved to be true:
I was there when Christ came back
But it wasn't at all what I had expected
I much preferred the hype

When we speak the words never come out right
Language fails and corrupts the idea
Like the music that ruined
the once pure words of this song
So forgive me if they have wasted your time
I just wish that we'd never spoken
And murdered the existing image that was before "Hello"
So please ignore the melody of this song
And don't speak another word
I'll pour us some Powers
And we can get down to business

(2010, *Under Judas Skies*)

SABOTEUR

Listen to the stars
And you'll think twice about whispering
All those sweet nothings you think of
For the starlit sky's a Judas
There's a knothole in the other room
It's not for looking in, but out
Your sister's making faces
Yes, you've failed to board it up

Listen to the crackling of the flames
As they swallow up the ransom note
You've written to yourself
Now the paper trail is gone
It's written in the sand
Lovely freedom
And they own every single grain
Listen to the sound of freedom –

Listen to the buzz
Here's a wrench; here's a spanner
For the works
Anywhere in the world
Where you gonna hide?
Listen to the stars up in the sky
While you can
Can you hear us?
Here's a wrench
A spanner
God bless
Goddamn

(2013, *Under Judas Skies*)

ŠVANKMAJER FILM IN 3D

When they nailed Him to the cross
When they pierced Him in the side
And you put your blindfold on
to get the firing squad to shoot
All the reporters and photographers
turned their attention to you
You had stolen the show
And then you whispered your name in our ears because
Everything is you

When the stars fell from the heavens
And rendered all love songs null and void
And the earth
It opened up and revealed the waving demons
Kicking and screaming
You were ready to drag us down with you
If our eyes were not all cast upon you
And so we learned your name by heart because
Everything is you

When the sun finally gave up and burnt out like a bulb
And all the priests could finally say, "We told you so!"
You started drinking gasoline to set yourself on fire
And we forgot about the sun and the darkness
that surrounded us
Now there's no need
to whisper your name in our ears because
Everything is you

(2012, *Under Judas Skies*)

CLOSING TIME (AMPERSANDS AND NIHIL)

Society Sue, who didn't know what to do,
Wandered off the edge of the world
With Calamity Jane, it's always the same,
They never even said their goodbyes

But the Devil's meditating on the numbers
And separating them into odd and even

And year after year
And fall after fall
Sue, she is still on my mind

Good morning to you, Miss Mary-Mid-Life-Crisis
Where do you go now from here?
Abandons ship, looks into the black light
And puts all her faith in the stars

But God is sitting in the basement
And has switched from Russian to Turkish roulette

Not for Him but for you
Just to see what happens
Though His lot may be put on the line

A treat just for you: a Punch and Judy peepshow
The professor is paving the way
Are you a 7 or 30, the Punch or the Judy?
Rock-paper-scissors: *Hurrah!*

And the Big Bang Operator
Has let all the chips fall where they may

Take control and create
Or do nothing and go
Where the winds have decided to take you

(2010, *Raygun Circus*)

LULLABY

Come inside
Leave your bones by the door
Step this way through the fire
The flames will do you good
Ignore what Kinski said
For the jungle's a terrible place
Just set your eyes to the sky
Don't fear the blue gates
Let the Katakuris lead you
Go softly, eyes to the sky
And go forth singing
Always singing at the foot of the volcano
Go lightly
Satan has come and is welcomed with open arms

A man finds solace in a bottle
That stores up the tears of a many misunderstood night
Waits in vain for a "plus one"
Who's been scratched off of the guest list for declaring
This Muzak is numbing
But it's out there for the taking
It's the virus that you download
The vodka for your loneliness
Yes, it's out there for the taking
It's the virus that you download
The vodka for your loneliness
Satan has come and is welcomed with open arms

Taint by number
The other side of the coin
The darkness over Celebration, Florida
The sinner and the saint
You need it
There is no one without the other
The gas mask and the suicide bomber
Go softly
There is no one without the other
So, ignore what Kinski said
For the jungle's a terrible place
But the morning will still come
Satan has come and is welcomed with open arms

(2014, *Raygun Circus*)

HOLOGRAMS

Skeleton hands pull the wings off of angels
For dancing on the head of a pin
He had grown tired of all of the chatter
"I'm as dead as dead can be!"

> The armory's empty,
> no guns left to fight with
> Stain the page with words,
> nothing new left to sing
> Leave your skin at the door;
> soak your brains in a barrel
> When your foot's in your mouth,
> every word's a sermon

Fifteen cats on a dead man's chest
Drink and fall and the Devil knows best
The yellow spring sky means it's time for the masks
Icha samcha and we all fall down

Up all night in a seedy motel room
Waiting for the dawn to break
Fifteen cats and the Devil knows best
Losing your train of thought

> The armory's empty,
> no guns left to fight with
> And down in the lab,
> there are no atoms left to split
> An uncovered secret is different tomorrow
> But every word's a sermon

(2012, "Holograms")

INTO THE BLACK

Heads will roll
The skies are falling
Time goes black
And here you are

The oceans drown
Angels clash
This is the time
To get it together

Black leather confused preacher listening
In the solitary confinement of confession
Looking for stiletto Christ in everything
Having to make do with all the silence

Apocalyptic
Voodoo doll
Stick a needle in its eye
And hope to die

Heads will roll
The heavens are collapsing
This is the time
To get it together

Cool like a razor – crucifix in your hand
Hanging on to it like a gun
And you think you've found a place
to rest your weary head
But you're sleeping in a barbed wire bed

(2014, "Prisoners / Into the Black")

AND THE HORSE YOU RODE IN ON

There will come a day when you realize
That everything that you have been doing
And everything that you've been up to until now
Has been nothing but a sham
A sick and twisted lie
The crumbling skull behind the smile
The sleight of hand that emptied the collection plate
And to all of those who've said
That they'd gone out for some milk
Or have gone out for a pack of smokes
and never came back
We say, "What the fuck!"
What the fuck
What the fuck
But everybody needs a fix
Some time or another

>And when the bough breaks
>And the cradle will fall
>We'll be waiting there for you
>Ready to do you in

And the disinfected hands with that extra scent of lemon
Will still be filthy no matter how hard you scrub
Like the trace of washed blood at the bottom of the drain
We'll find you out
We'll find you out
The spit in the eye
And the kick in the balls
The it's-not-you-it's-me/s
And the what-if-they-made-it-all-ups
We may fall on deaf ears
But in the end, you bet your life, we'll find you out
We'll find you out
But forgive us our trespasses
And lead us to temptation
Cause everybody needs a fix
Some time or another

  And when the bough breaks
  And the cradle will fall
  We'll still be waiting there for you
  We'll still be ready to do you in

(2010, *Into the Black*)

ONE MAN'S POISON

Do not speak
Do not write anything down
Sew the mouth shut
Dr. Guillotine's in town

Silence is obedience
Silence is obedience
Bow down to obedience
Only know obedience

Do not speak
Do not reach out to the world
Take this sword
It is mightier than the pen

We are kings (authority!)
We are kings (authority!)
Iron fist (authority!)
We are kings (authority!)

Kamikaze fighters
Nosedive into Heaven
Nothing's shocking
As a million hits are reached

Voyeurs in a vacuum!
Voyeurs in a vacuum!
Voyeurs in a vacuum!
Voyeurs in a vacuum!

Do not leave
From the comfort of your home
Kick your feet up
Watch the guts fall to the floor

Living in a snuff film
Voyeurs in a snuff film
Living in a snuff film
Every day's a snuff film

(2015, *Into the Black*)

ALL THE BLESSINGS YOU CAN GET

The word from up above is law
That which was shall be again
The world turned upside down
17 seconds
Then you're down
Sink or swim
Stay underground
Keep the camera on the crowd
And a searchlight in the dark
To keep you in your place
Sound the alarm if someone talks
Make that call if you suspect

Resist, reject, and undermine
Truth or lie
The ties that bind
Your own you own
We're here to find the missing link
Put it together, and then bang!
Hand over heart; hand on the book
Something to slaughter
Take the oath
Shadows curtsy on the walls
We know where you lay your head
So take this hand

(2016, *Into the Black*)

GOING OUT WITH A BANG

Kiss the paper-thin Christ
Taste the blood in the wine

     Knick knack paddy whack
     Pocket full of stones
     Fessing up to sins committed
     Making room for more

In a holy city
In a lonely city
In the sacred city
Where Denial leads the blind

Kiss the paper-thin Christ
Drink five bottles of wine
     Knick knack paddy whack…

Poke out those eyes
Cut out your heart
Chop off your head
There's no need for those anymore

Punish your reflexes
Deny your natural instincts
Gouge out those eyes
For you're in the hands of God
     Knick knack paddy whack…

Kiss the paper-thin Christ
Drinking all of the wine

In a holy city
In a lonely city
In the sacred city
Where anything fools the blind

Values and morals –
Inventions of man
Define your own concepts
Define your own life

Enjoy what you can
For soon you'll be dust
Take it or leave it
Cause you can't bring it with you in the end

Sin is subject to change
Do what you want
Spit on the cross:
Spit! Spit! Spit!

     Knick knack paddy whack…

     Knick knack paddy whack
     Pocket full of nails
     Bringing out the best in you
     Crucify your foes

Burn the paper-thin Christ
Passing out on the floor

(2009, *Into the Black*)

TERMINAL FICTION

We went up to the hill
To see what's been happening there
There's people rolling down the hill
Getting up and doing it again

Went up on that hill
Made sure to stay out of sight
They're clawing at each other's throats
As if it were an eye for an eye

They're tearing pages out of books
And replacing them with ransom notes
Set fire to the evidence
And put the ashes in an urn

Now two and two make five
What once was dead is now alive
And there's a massacre where no one died
Gone but never forgotten

Look up to the sky
Will you remember what you'll see today?
Some say light rain; some say cloudy
But the weathermen shrug their shoulders

Up on the hill
There's no such thing as lies
Just people rolling down over broken glass
And a ton of ashes put in urns

(2017, "DNA Parade / Terminal Fiction")

SWIFTLY INTO THE NIGHT

When you came to your senses
Everything was the same
No blackout lasts forever
And the world's still in flames

Keep your voice down
Or you'll give us away
But why bother to whisper
When we know it's the end?

No Infinity Waltzes
And the singer is dead
Play that sonata backwards
To reverse everything

But you'll come to your senses
And that day will not come
Bring the cup to your lips
So you know it's the end

(2016, "Swiftly into the Night")

TRUTH DECAY

From the lips of men
And the skulls of men
Take these words and thoughts and manipulate
Cry foul
Cry wolf
The only truth's in your mind
Form a new history to suit you
To have them believe
The only way to believe
Leave your unsigned message in a bottle
In a sea of rust
Unfiltered code
Can't tell the zeroes from the ones

Guilty by assimilation
Put the fly in the ointment
Information rodeo
Don't know what's up from down
Fingerprints in a private vacuum
Where true sympathies lie

Guilty by annihilation
Wash the lies from your lips
Sweet-nothings intimidation
Stick your tongue in your ear
Guilty by annihilation
The damage is done

(2017, *The Treachery of Truth*)

REIGN OF ERROR

Pit stops through time
Stealing through the ages
Ransacking Newton's room
Come back a savior
Avoid amnesia
No need for the marches
Protect from this alchemy
That turns wine into piss

The sky splits in two
And the stars go rogue
Who gets the wine?
Who gets the poison?
The truth that you've held so dear's
Now been replaced
But be sure it's the bomb
That will bring us together

(2017, *The Treachery of Truth*)

COME CLEAN

The left hand don't know
What the right hand is doing
Good health to you
Death to all!
Conspire in secret
To set up this mess
Cut off both arms
To pay for the cure

Behind closed doors
The strait-jacket fits
Pen in mouth
Drool the words onto the page
With a Yo! and a Ho!
And it's down we go
Cut off both legs
To pay for the cure

(2017, *The Treachery of Truth*)

CASTAWAYS

Speak but do not say the words
That should be mouthed
Without a sound
If you want to remember
For in a day they won't exist
The rats have left the sinking ship
Into the sea
They've had enough
Yes, even all the loyal ones
Have flung themselves
Into the brine

Hoist the flag and put your faith in lunacy,
Conspiracy,
And a show of farce
Demands for the captain's head
Drowned out his rants:
This mutiny does not exist!
Came the decree
But no one listened
The rats have left the burning ship
And we follow close behind

(2017, *The Treachery of Truth*)

SEVEN WORDS

Over the distant horizon
Looking for the edge of the world
With a sense and with a purpose
Who says the world isn't flat
Treasonous facts
Hail the blacklist!
Punishment kiss and the will of God
Follow the breadcrumbs to the war
The alphabet does not exist
Superstition avalanche
Deliver us from evidence
Go go Johnny, go go Johnny
There you go in the name of the Lord

Double standards before your eyes
If it doesn't fit, then it never happened
Reality is elastic
Give it a go and we'll all fit in
Praises for amnesia
Fantasy world and the lay of the land
Follow the breadcrumbs to the war
Number system conspiracy
This is the sound of a 45
Spun on repeat and repeat and repeat
Go go Johnny, go go Johnny
There you go with the fear of God

(2017, *The Treachery of Truth*)

REALITY LIMBO

Hail to the king!
Hail to the king!
Hail to the king of nothing!

Stranger than fiction
Delusion addiction
A knock on the door
And Ubu shows you in
Sucked into a bad dream
Nothing is what it seems
Sanity assassins
Hallucination agents
Hard at work and obscene
For the good of the people
And it's hail to the king
To the king of nothing

Babble and fiction
Second-rate diction
Omit and distort
Then repeat and repeat
Where did the past go?
Before it was hijacked
It's not in your mind
And it's not there in history
Pardon the killers
Hard at work for the people
And to Hell with the king
And the horse he road in on

(2017, *The Treachery of Truth*)

UNCOLLECTED LYRICS
AND WORDS

MUSIC MACHINE

Juggling coins in a zeppelin with holes
Who's going to drop the bomb?
Play out of key to remember the one
Who leapt onto another train
Samurai sword in his hand, walks the streets
"Your songs are much too long"
Pay your respects to nostalgia with money
Carbon copies are just as good

Bureaucratic inclinations
"Apply now!" to sing your song
Die for your art when you're lost in the labyrinth
Without a nickel to your name
Our scientists have cloned your DNA structure
You're no longer needed here
Capitalist authority
Free deodorant stick!

Soldiers of culture for the upcoming Reich
Like penguins in their suits
Who's going to play my harp when I'm gone?
This is business!
Digital war in an auditorium
The soundtracks are all the same
Corpses of men in a junkyard of filth
Too much to filter out

Italia – classical harmony
Even in dissonance
Loading the gun with a tuning fork
Barb wired melody
Smashed in the face with mnemonic devices
Repeat after me: repeat after me!
Formulas work much better than blood
Mathematicians – Amen!

(2000)

SALVATION FROM A VENDING MACHINE

This is not Nirvana!

Trespass
Hollow it father who
Hoo hoo hoo
Hoot, the owl
No!
As into those Usus in kingdom temptation
Daily cum
Forgive
We and our Bee
Our trespasses
Us
But –

Please enter correct change

Day *böse maldito*
Who give earth
<Done>
Heaven lead us against nothing and Bee
Bread will forgive
        <balls of foam gently dropped upon a lazily
        perched pane of glass – one baby blue, the other a
        dark rose color>
Our thigh is thine art
Amen
A looked over thigh from –
Name Heaven –
        <banging on two pieces of wood: 2 x 4's to be
        exact>
– As this delivers us

This machine only accepts nickels

A 1970s film festival
A memory of Stephen
Staples in the head
Science fiction pinball machine massage
Looking up
The oxygen swallowed Karlheinz Stockhausen
Heaven is for little German kids
Lambs in the meadow:
  "Wir singen nichts!"
No money today
Cowbell insulation
Crash and pops
1970
5 after 0
Back to 01
Waiting for *Kontakte*
Warten

(2001)

WHAT A SHAME

Nothing special
Someone poured mercury in my tea
In the bar
We talk a lot in the bar
The old widow laughs
A one-eyed angel dances on the table
He earns the money
And we take it
Then we shoot him with harpoons
We needed the money
We always talk
Always and often
And always is often
There is no gold here for us
Here, money is like fornication
Well, then...

(2002)

THREE PAWNS

Unfolded
The Queen of Tarts rejects
And all the money's
Flushed down the sewer
In the court
The jesters run the streets
While the garden vegetables
Dream away the night

Down the stairs
The Morning After Girl escapes
In the wallet
The moths pour out like water
Her emotions
Flattered by the anvil
In the room
Respectability rolls off the side of the bed

In the city
The clowns remove their scars
And the tears
Are buried deep inside their shoes
In a play
Where dress rehearsals don't exist
No one's a star
Nobody even found the stage

(2002, T.O.E.)

POMME

Don't hiccup in my face
Because your smoke-filled rosary…
The pages of the book get sodden
And the neighbors squelch

The candle flame leaps to another chord
No one's jealous except for the tune
But, no…
Not yet…
Another time!
Tonight's the time we beg for treats

CHORUS:
Chairs! Chairs!
Can we have the music?
We don't know who is to blame

Chairs! Chairs!
Make it quick
Before the game's all done

Up the stairs
The bellows heave
The string – it breaks
But we don't mind

Enunciation
Our better half
But, just remember
Potatoes don't make for loving kings

CHORUS

(2002, T.O.E.)

REJECTION

Hundreds of them fell from the sky
Wooden blocks in an assortment of colors and characters
      – letters, numbers and kana alike – showered upon
      her like an avalanche of celebratory confetti
Arms raised to protect her face
This unfortunate,
yet spectacular display of color could be seen for blocks
Amidst the towering skyscrapers and hot afternoon sun
Of this busy downtown quarter
Yet no such consequence was imparted to anyone else
For each individual existed within his or her own universe

She lay toppled beneath the pile of bricks
Although the sidewalk had become blocked
Nobody seemed to notice
Struggling as she crawled out
She moved her lips, but no words came out
Try as she might
She had failed to convey the simple meaning of "help"
Finally
She managed to crawl out of her wreckage
And bring the back of her wrist up against her cheek
To wipe away the drops of blood from a cut
That had
Since surfacing
Begun to glint in the hot sun…

(2004)

                – introduction to "Nursery Rhyme"

ALL THOUGHTS TURN TO STONE (A WOODCUT)

Ali pulled the key back out of the slot
into which it had been inserted
He had changed his mind
In fact
This has happened before on several occasions
This was all he had left
It's what kept him going lately
This and a bottle of whiskey
What lies behind that door? he'd wonder
"Nobody knows how to sing 'em these days..."

At such moments
He could have embarked on his very own trip
Into the end of the night

The bottle falls and shatters on the tile floor
Silence

But now, there's just no way of knowing...

(2004)

– introduction to "When All Is Said and Done at The
End of The Night"

BORN OF FRUSTRATION

The shape of the crowd at the top of the hill
Resembles a piece of sculpture
Commemorating the defeat of some enemy
During some war
At some time
With banners and flags held up high

Amidst the green grass
It resembles the Laocoön
With faces straight out of a Bruegel
They're shouting, "Wickertank, wickertank!"
With the white flag blowing strongly in the wind

And so, the procession bustles through the meadow
So that everyone may hear
And there's even music, dancing, and singing
For the best is yet to come
And there's no turning back
Wickertank, wickertank, wickertank...
And yet, for all that merriment
Those were the only words I could hear

(2004)

– introduction to "Kokeshi Doll"

IT'S A CURSE!

Paranoia man!
These are his notes
Scribbled on the floor
During those unwelcome hours of the night
Alternating between the pen and the bottle
Between empty rooms and the swill
Toss and turn in a drunken state
And so, the bourbon ain't your friend
Paranoia man!
It's time to go
For the sun is beginning to knock
On the door
Of this beautifully filthy
House of scum

(2005)

— introduction to "Paranoia Man in a House of Scum"

STEAL THIS SONG

A child sits and waits for his mother to come
With a silver spoon and a bottle full of poison
You know, he's at that impressionable age
With the sun prying open the blinds with a crow bar
Offering candy and a slap on the wrist, saying:
Here's your daily dose of lullabies, son

He'll sing for you

Scum and disease ooze from the jukebox
And we're staring with faces like broken windows
Anticipating what today will bring
I can't remember yesterday
I've got too many three-verse songs written down
So give your money to the Lorelei girls, who say:

We'll sing for you
And the sailors sink into the sea

A glimmer of hope from the wild blue yonder
Missed the tunnels of chaos, but it's *slowly but surely*
One of these days, he's going to get it just right
Looks straight into the eye of the beast
at the gate holding keys
Ready to strike
Can you imagine how we felt when we saw the white flag?

And we cried:
Shut it out of our vision!
Shut it out of our minds!
Shut it out of our senses!
Shut it all out!

We'll sing for you
Smiles on their lips, the sailors sank into the sea

A glimmer of hope from the wild blue yonder
Now could you ever imagine
how we felt when we saw that flag?

(2007)

INSTANT SONG

I heard that you had recently lost your mind
Dialing 911 with your finger poised above the final "one"
The crossword puzzle solved itself
You're not used to having options
Like walking down the snake market
and checking out the vendors
Like those girls behind the Hello Kitty curtains
And the tennis shoes all sealed up tight in plastic
By the fortune tellers, turtle heads,
And the python that the children pet
You know, they say that the soup is good for men

And you had taken the numbers apart in my head
Like you were pulling apart the stitches in your leg
Those numbers that I had arranged so very neatly
Taken apart one by one
And you had made your decision
Then the universe exploded
But I too had made my own
Without ever even realizing
Now I'm sorting out the alphabet
I pick up all of Einstein's dreams
Put the pieces in the trash bin
So I don't cut my bare feet
And I'll think about the next song that I'll write
With the line about a sports team
Like the one I heard this evening
Or perhaps about a town that I have never been to
But I'll make it sound as if I have

But that song is not for singing
And the water's not for drinking
And no, *sundae* isn't ice cream
And the gun, it ain't for shooting
And your Jesus ain't for saving
Like the whiskey ain't for healing
No, this song is not for singing
It's just another one of my unfinished songs

(2009)

FICTION PANIC

At the edge of the world
In a lonely hotel room
With the incense and fruit
And porn on TV
None of the comforts of home
But the magic had made sense
Then they sent in the SWAT team
When the sky had fallen

You wanted to believe in
A fairy tale of your own
You needed to believe in
Something to hold on to

A world view up on trial
Nothing is as it seems
The rug pulled out from under
Kicking away the chair

You needed to believe
Kicking away the chair
A fairy tale of your own
Kicking away the chair
A fairy tale of your own
Kicking away the chair
A fairy tale not your own
Kicking away the chair
Kicking away the chair…

Jack pushed Jill down the hill
But there are safer ways around town
Don't get so sentimental
This is the time of your life
Take a cab into town
Have your last taste of gin
But don't get so sentimental
This is the time of your life

(2013, Tactical Fever)

ALL THE KING'S HORSES

When the door is closed
That's when all the festivities begin
The scribbled madness
And the wandering thoughts –
Who wrote the one about
the brutal and vicious human chess game in the East?
Yes, that's right
Something about kings…

The temperature rises
And things get uncomfortable
Before they start to get comfortable
And the innocent child
Is thrown out the window
Again
We'll have to put it off for tomorrow
Again
We've got darkness and oblivion to contemplate for now
While there's still time
While there's still…

(consciousness)

And all the split-second regrets
Are forgotten the morning after
When the door is closed
And the festivities have begun

(2013)

REGGIE

Lost in Yokohama
The stranger had found himself
Washed up on a beach on the Pacific Coast
With a message that he'd brought
Not in a bottle,
For the bottle was for companionship,
But on his lips
He had waited for so long to say:
"If you're drowning, then you must come up for air"

Six in the morning
Down the same streets once again
Glaring music from the night clubs
And the drunks will always keep you company
The spring sky's a bright orange
And the acid rain stains your shoes again
But the sudden air raid sirens
And the motorcycle chase
Provide some entertainment
To break up the monotony
When the theater is on fire
Then you know it's time to leave

The end of days has come
And it's pounding on the door
You never believed
But now you're on your knees
It's a desperate measure taken
When you want to raise the dead
And if you're drowning
Disappear into the sea
A last defiant gesture
To a hostile world

(2014)

INDEX OF TITLES

A

B

C

D

F

G

ABOUT THE AUTHOR

Adolf N.S. is the writer, vocalist, and guitarist for Raygun Circus. A multi-instrumentalist who also records and produces his own music, he also wrote and recorded solo music as A.N.S. and Cori Celesti. He has also played with Tactical Fever and Street of Little Girls. Other past bands and collaborations include T.O.E. and The Marauding Band of Cut-Throats. *Terminal Fiction* is his first book.

www.rayguncircus.com